D0208953

NOTES FOR PROFESSIONAL LIBRARIANS
AND LIBRARY USERS

This is an original book title published by The Haworth Pastoral Press®, an imprint of The Haworth Press, Inc. Unless otherwise noted in specific chapters with attribution, materials in this book have not been previously published elsewhere in any format or language.

CONSERVATION AND PRESERVATION NOTES

All books published by The Haworth Press, Inc. and its imprints are printed on certified pH neutral, acid free book grade paper. This paper meets the minimum requirements of American National Standard for Information Sciences-Permanence of Paper for Printed Material, ANSI Z39.48-1984.

Pastoral Care to Muslims
Building Bridges

THE HAWORTH PASTORAL PRESS
Rev. James W. Ellor, DMin, DCSW, CGP
Melvin A. Kimble, PhD
Co-Editors in Chief

Aging and Spirituality: Spiritual Dimensions of Aging Theory, Research, Practice, and Policy edited by David O. Moberg

Wu Wei, *Negativity, and Depression: The Principle of Non-Trying in the Practice of Pastoral Care* by Siroj Sorajjakool

Pastoral Care to Muslims: Building Bridges by Neville A. Kirkwood

Pastoral Care to Muslims
Building Bridges

Neville A. Kirkwood, DMin

The Haworth Pastoral Press®
An Imprint of The Haworth Press, Inc.
New York • London • Oxford

Published by

The Haworth Pastoral Press®, an imprint of The Haworth Press, Inc., 10 Alice Street, Binghamton, NY 13904-1580.

Cover design by Jennifer M. Gaska.

Library of Congress Cataloging-in-Publication Data

Kirkwood, Neville A.
    Pastoral care to Muslims : building bridges / Neville A. Kirkwood.
        p. cm.
    Includes bibliographical references and index.
    ISBN 0-7890-1476-9 (alk. paper)—ISBN 0-7890-1477-7 (alk. paper)
    1. Islam—Doctrines. 2. Church work with the sick. 3. Muslims—Pastoral counseling of.
4. Care of the sick—Religious aspects—Islam. 5. Christianity and other religions—Islam.
6. Islam—Relations—Christianity. I. Title

BP165.5 .K57 2001
261.2'7—dc21

2001024390

CONTENTS

ABOUT THE AUTHOR

Neville A. Kirkwood, DMin, is an author, lecturer, and preacher, and has served in cross-cultural missions in India for seventeen years and as a hospital chaplain for eighteen years. He earned his doctorate at the San Francisco Theological Seminary in San Anselmo, California. Dr. Kirkwood has served in many capacities, including as President of the Australian College of Chaplains and Chairperson of the Civil Chaplaincies Advisory Committee of NSW. He has authored several books, including *A Hospital Handbook on Multiculturalism and Religion, Independent India's Troubled North-East: 1952-1969,* and the 1996 Australian Christian Book of the Year, *Pastoral Care in Hospitals.*

Foreword

People of the Muslim faith are urged toward caring for the sick, the disabled, the elderly, widows, and orphans. It is a religious duty.

In his book *Pastoral Care to Muslims,* Dr. Neville A. Kirkwood has succeeded in transmitting the values and principles of the Muslim faith in a clear and distinguished style. The level of research and work conducted by Dr. Kirkwood is impressive. The book is a practical guide that will increase the understanding of Muslim needs in hospitals.

While reading the various chapters of the book, I have learned (in some instances for the first time) religious matters that are of more immediate importance than the routine exigencies of secular life. This book will be instrumental for many years to come in the work performance of doctors, health care workers, nurses, and hospital chaplains (Inshaallah). On behalf of the Australian Muslim Community, I congratulate and thank Dr. Kirkwood for this valuable contribution.

May Allah bless all of us!

Ali Roude, OAM
Chairman, Islamic Council of New South Wales

* * *

Australia may be in a unique position to make a significant contribution to harmonious relationships between the great world religions, and so to world peace. Our short history and our evolving culture seem at present to favor tolerance and acceptance of diversity, not just in patterns of social behavior but also in patterns of religious belief. Australia is not burdened by a history of conflict between peoples or religions, with the exception of the tragic history of European treatment of indigenous Australians. Perhaps we have learned by that sad experience to be more tolerant of recently arrived cultural and linguistic groups and representatives of other world religions.

Whatever the roots of this easy acceptance and general tolerance that marks Australian society, it is something to be treasured and protected from anything that would undermine or unravel it. Moreover, if it is to last, it must be constantly deepened by more profound philosophical and theological undergirding. In this context, Dr. Kirkwood has produced a remarkable work. He, a Protestant Christian clergyman, has written a work acceptable to Muslims on the pastoral care to be extended to them by Christian pastoral workers in health care facilities.

Dr. Kirkwood is to be congratulated for the care with which he has interpreted the Islamic religious experience and theology to others and the sensitivity with which he has outlined an appropriate pastoral response on the part of those who are not Muslims to patients in Australian health care facilities. He has shown that it is possible to be a committed Christian while at the same time being respectful of the Muslim faith and attentive to this population's pastoral needs when they are patients in our hospitals. His work is a real service to those concerned with such pastoral care in any country where Muslims are now a significant presence in health care facilities.

Michael Putney, DD
Auxiliary Bishop, Catholic Archdiocese
Brisbane

Preface

At the outset certain limitations should be acknowledged. In any religion there are a number of schools of theological thought and interpretations of the revelations, history, and myths. In a book of this compass it is not possible to delve into the theological debates that have raged over centuries. Any introduction of a religion to the uninitiated must be content to give a general background of its belief and practice.

In considering Islam, the first acknowledgement must be the Qur'an, or Koran, which contains what Muslims believe are the revelations of God directly given to the Prophet Mohammed through the archangel Gabriel. These are the scriptures revered by all Muslims. It should be noted that Muslims consider only the Arabic text to be the Qur'an. Translations have not the same authenticity. Throughout this work the translation of the Qur'an used is in the Penguin Classic Series translated by N.J. Dawood, 1995 edition. As with all translations of scriptures it must be expected that there will be discrepancies among translators as to the meaning and transliteration of certain words of the original language— in this case, Arabic. Many words have no equivalent meaning in other languages. My intention in quoting from the Qur'an is that the reader may be able to grasp some of the basic beliefs of Islam from the scriptures themselves.

It is impossible to confine all the theology and doctrine of Islam in a book of this size. The issues highlighted are those that are likely to surface in the minds of patients and/or their relatives within the hospital context. Even within these perimeters, all aspects cannot be explored. Here the effort has been made to convey some understanding of the average Muslim's position. A bibliography is included which may be used for further reading.

In a personal communication, Imam Asaroglu wrote, "It is understood that there are not many reliable resources available in

Australia as much as there is in Muslim Countries. The opposite applies to Christian sources."

For the reader requiring a deeper study it may have been helpful to include the Arabic text of the quotations along with the translations. This was not considered necessary, as the readers, generally, would not be literate in the Arabic language. Also, this book is not intended to be an intense theological dissertation.

The Arabic language differentiates between God (i.e., Allah) the God of Abraham, and the god/gods who are worshipped by nonbelievers in the God of Abraham, Isaac, and Jacob. Muslims refer to him as "Allah." As it is assumed that many readers will be Christians and Jews, Allah will be referred to as God throughout. This is to stress our mutuality in identifying with the God of Abraham. Thus when God with a capital G appears it will refer to Allah. Without a capital, other deities will be the point of reference.

In the preparation for this book I am indebted to the Islamic Council of New South Wales, Imam Abdurrahaman Asaroglu, Ali Roude, Bakar Pooloo, and Arif Agnu. My good friend Richard Seary, who perused the original draft, offered valuable comments, which have been included. Peter and Denise Hocken-Venning vetted the final draft. Twenty years ago, Ray Register and his Muslim friends in Nazareth provided many insights, which have been retained.

This book is dedicated to the promotion of peace and harmony among peoples in the very intolerant world of the twenty-first century.

Introduction

Health care institutions worldwide are increasingly becoming aware of the need to practice holistic medicine. This covers physical, mental, social, and spiritual components of the patient for effective recovery. The history of hospital practice has seen the purely physical approach to medicine extend to mental health by the employment of psychiatrists and, later, psychologists. Awareness of the effect of social background became relevant, so first almoners and, more recently, social workers, joined hospital staffs.

Over the past fifty years religious and health authorities have become conscious that in many cases the spiritual and religious uncertainties often mitigate against the maximum recovery of the patient. Christian churches are increasingly providing chaplains and pastoral care workers to provide support and spiritual assurances to the patient and a nonmedical ally on the staff for the patient.

Where competent, trained chaplains are appointed to separate units of the hospital they are often invited to become part of the clinical team. As team members they are expected to make their contributions to the planning, treatment, and management of the patient. At times, because of additional information passed on by the patient or relatives, a chaplain influences diagnosis and treatment.

Hospital staff appreciate the addition of a chaplain to their unit. They have one person with an expertise different from their own, in whom they can place confidence and treat with professional equity in relation to specific aspects concerning a patient. Each unit in a hospital has particular protocols, treatment programs, and equipment for their patients. The ward pastoral caregiver understands the differing activities of the unit and the stress faced by patients in that unit. Through this interface, the patient is able to receive the appropriate pastoral attention. The staff also are able to receive the support they need from the chaplain who assists them in the care of the patient. Experience has shown that patients respond more to the person whose face they see daily or at least several times a week. A weekly visit does not allow the same rapport to build up. Such pastoral visitors are not readily available when the patient faces a crisis or critical decision making.

Access to a person from his or her own particular faith should be offered to the patient. The chaplain is not there to convert or divert patients from their chosen or hereditary religious position. Hospital patients are often absorbed with their own physical condition, the need to get better, or to deal with other issues arising from their illness. At such a time, efforts to intrude religious or theological debate is irritating and counterproductive. Many religiously tunnel-visioned visitors claim bedside conversions, about which they boast. Patients have reported to chaplains that to say "Yes" was the easiest way to muzzle the badgering they were experiencing. The appointed pastoral person is there to provide the spiritual support that the patient is able to accept; spiritual support that does not conflict with the patient's own religious affiliations.

As Islam is one of the two fastest-growing religions (Buddhism is the other), the population of Muslim patients in hospitals around the world is increasing. The migratory possibilities of modern times make this highly probable.

Consequently, pastoral care workers need to have confidence when meeting Muslim patients in their wards. That confidence will come only as they understand the faith perspectives of their patients. It is most important to remember that they worship the God of Abraham as do Jews and Christians.

My own encounters with Muslim patients and their relatives have been personally and spiritually enriching for me as the pastoral caregiver. Many Muslims have a deeper awareness and devotion to God than do many of those representing other faiths. While the chaplain's role is to offer pastoral care, frequently the patient also gives much in return. Such was the nature of the relationship between a migrant Arab Muslim cancer patient named Ali and myself. Mention will be made of him in Chapters 3 and 4.

The following pages are intended to enable mutuality in spiritual care and understanding to be experienced by both caregiver and patient.

SECTION I:
THE MUSLIM MIND

Chapter 1

Why Muslims?

By the year C.E. 2005, 25 percent of the world's population will be followers of Islam. The Western world is becoming more aware of increasing numbers of Muslims in their communities. This growth of the Muslim population in our areas will increase with natural procreation, conversion, and migration from overcrowded lands with declining prospects. Also, many Muslims migrate in order to be reunited with family members.

Many Christians in the West have negative attitudes toward Muslims for a number of reasons. Muslim-majority countries are in Asia and Africa. Because of the West's colonialist, patronizing, and imperialistic mentality from the Middle Ages up to a generation or two ago, the peoples from these countries were considered inferior. Evangelical missionary activities viewed all non-Christians as heathens or pagans. This type of thinking is still prevalent, particularly among middle-aged and older Christians.

Christians generally have promoted an antagonistic attitude toward Muslims by critically and self-righteously publicizing some extreme practices, especially in relation to women. I have personally been close to some of those actions and denounced them. Fanatical and extreme behavior are often not condoned by the Qur'an. We Christians seem to so easily forget that many similar repugnant acts by so-called Christians are daily reported in the press of Christian-majority countries. Muslim periodicals, rightly, are constantly warning their young people not to fall into the ways of the decadent permissive spirit found in many Christian-majority countries.

Forty years ago I was talking with two Muslims, one who worked as a cook and the other as a bearer in the home of an English businessman residing in Calcutta. Their answer to my inquiry concerning their understanding of Christians was alarming: "All Christians drink alcohol, get drunk, and swap wives." This was a generalization of the observed lifestyle of many so-called Christians, largely commercial or diplomatic representatives from Western countries, particularly Britain. They were "accidental" Christians by virtue of birth and parenting. Such does not make a person devout. My defense of the faith had little effect. Their personal eyewitness evidence was irrefutable to them. The fact that so many expatriates lived this way was well known. This left little wind in my sails.

Let us first acknowledge that the frequent writings by a member of one religion concerning the activities and beliefs of another religion most likely will be biased and distorted. My research into many religions has led me to prefer authors who are disciples of the religion about which they are writing. In my experience in seminary and elsewhere, Christian writers and missionaries so corrupted the facts of the other religion about which they were writing or speaking that I have come to the conclusion that it is almost impossible to observe objectively the religion in the field. It is now possible to question whether truth was evident in the material I was taught. An example of this was the consistent relating that Mohammed was a lecherous fanatic. In understanding the life and cultural practices of the time, an objective observer must see him as a person of integrity, sincerity, and moral uprightness in both sexual and spiritual matters.

Second, in the story of the good neighbor, Jesus pointed out that the Pharisee and the priest who ignored the injured fellow Jew were not the wounded man's neighbors. It was the foreigner, the nonworshipper in the synagogue, who proved to be the neighbor. The parable's title, "The Good Samaritan," says it all.

A research program that I undertook produced a set of guidelines for the care of Muslims in the hospital. These guidelines form the crux of this book. As part of the fieldtesting I sent the guidelines to the clergy and chaplains who visited a particular hospital where 54 percent of the patients were Muslims. They were requested to use these in offering pastoral care to the Muslim patients when it was appropriate to do so. At the end of three months they were forwarded an evaluation questionnaire. To my amazement and disbelief not one of these clergy or chaplains had visited a Muslim patient. One made the comment that he did not consider it part of his ministry to visit Muslims. How contrary to the spirit of Jesus!

These priests, who had three months of opportunity for offering pastoral care to 54 percent of the patients, walked down the other side of those hospital wards. Many of those patients would have been crying out for some spiritual support and comfort. So many of them needed someone who would be able to apply the touch of a caring and merciful God. One chaplain at another hospital, however, gained enough confidence from the exercise that he worked with a Buddhist and commented that the guidelines worked for more than Muslims.

Third, in offering pastoral care to Muslims we are offering the tenderness of the same God. Jews, Christians, and Muslims worship the God of Abraham, Isaac, and Jacob. The Jews call him Yahweh in Hebrew. The Christians call him God. The Muslims, in Arabic, worship "Allah."

The Koran (Qur'an) is the sacred scripture of Islam. The spelling Qur'an is more acceptable in academic circles. The phonetic spelling Koran ensures a more accurate pronunciation and recognition. Mohammed is accepted as the medium of divine will as expressed in the Koran. From C.E. 610 until his death on June 8, C.E. 632, Mohammed received a series of revelations from God through the archangel Gabriel. These he memorized and taught his followers, who also committed them to memory. Later they were written down by his followers and collated in present form under Uthman, the third caliph to succeed Mohammed as leader of Islam (C.E. 644-656). All previous copies of the Koran were destroyed. (After the death of Mohammed, caliphs followed him in the leadership of Islam.)

The basic teachings of the Koran have strong similarities to Jewish and Christian teaching. An example of this is the first sura (chapter) of the Koran, Fatihah, which are the last words a dying person should hear and are part of the daily prayers.

Sura 1. "Fatihah"

Praise be to God, Lord of the Universe,
The Compassionate, The Merciful,
Sovereign of the Day of Judgment!
You alone we worship,
To you alone we turn for help.
Guide us to the straight Path,
The Path of those whom you have favored,
Not those who have incurred your wrath,
Nor those who have gone astray.

As Christians can we fault these words? Jews would find similar thoughts in the Psalms.

Mohammed's first wife Khadijah, whom he loved and admired deeply, had a Christian background. During his days as the leader of a caravan working the trade routes to the countries of the Levant (Transjoran, Lebanon, Syria, and Palestine) he sought to understand Christianity. However, what he found were Christians who were worshipping statues and involved in some occultist pagan rituals and practices. The fifth and sixth centuries C.E. were dark periods in the history of the Church. In many areas of Christianity, the true spirit of Jesus the Christ was difficult to find. The Prophet's (peace be upon him) mission indicates some of that disappointment. The Koran makes a number of critical references as well as positive references to the "People of the Book," as he called Christians. Some of those negative remarks are entirely appropriate in the light of the condition of the church of the day. His warnings must be taken in the light of the prevailing religious history. We must ask ourselves—if a new Mohammed should arise in these days, would the West's so-called portrayal of Christian living be worthy of similar correction?

The Koran also makes repeated reference to Jesus as a prophet and apostle of God. It holds Jesus as one of the principal servants of God, including calling him the Messiah in the account of the annunciation of Mary:

The angels said to Mary: "God bids you rejoice in a Word from Him. His name is the Messiah, Jesus son of Mary. He shall be noble in this world and in the hereafter, and shall be one of those who are favored. He shall preach to men in his cradle and in the prime of manhood, and shall lead a righteous life." (S. 3:45-46)

In further describing the Mission of Jesus it attributes to him these words:

By God's leave, I shall heal the blind and the leper, and raise the dead to life. I shall tell you what to eat and what to store in your houses. Surely, that will be a sign for you, if you are true believers. I come to confirm the Torah, which preceded me, and to make lawful some of the things you are forbidden. I bring you a sign from your Lord: therefore fear God and obey me. God is my Lord and your Lord: therefore serve Him. That is the straight path. (S. 3:48-51)

Similar words are found in the nonbiblical "Gospel of Thomas."

The Koran is quick to point out the humanity of Jesus:

The Messiah, the son of Mary, was no more than an apostle: other apostles passed away before him. His mother was a saintly woman. They both ate earthly food. (S. 5:75)

In speaking to Christians it further says:

People of the Book! Do not transgress the bounds of truth in your religion. Do not yield to desires of those who have erred before you; who themselves have strayed from the even path.

Those of the Israelites who disbelieved were cursed by David and Jesus, the son of Mary, because they rebelled and committed evil. Nor did they censure themselves for any wrong they did. Evil were their deeds. (S. 5:77-78)

Also according to the Koran, the Gospel was given to Jesus by God with a warning to his followers to obey it:

After them We sent forth Jesus, son of Mary, confirming the Torah already revealed, and gave him the Gospel, in which there is guidance and light, corroborating what was revealed before in the Torah, a guide and an admonition to the righteous. Therefore let those who follow the Gospel judge according to what God has revealed therein. Evil doers are those who do not judge according to God's revelations. (S. 5:46-47)

The followers of God who surrender to him are acceptable to him:

They say: "Accept the Jewish or the Christian faith and you shall be rightly guided."

Say: "By no means! We believe in the faith of Abraham the upright one. He was no idolater."

Say: "We believe in God and that which was revealed to us; in what was revealed to Abraham, Ishmael, Isaac, Jacob, and the tribes; to Moses and Jesus and the other prophets by their Lord. We make no distinction among any of them, and to God we have surrendered ourselves."

If they accept your faith, they shall be rightly guided; if they reject it, they shall surely be in schism. Against them God is your all-sufficient defender. He hears all and knows all." (S. 2:135-137)

Here we are to understand that it is not the following of a creed or a faith such as the Torah or the principles of Sermon on the Mount but only the complete surrender to God that is vital.

Muslims are warned about friendship with Jews and Christians:

Believers take neither Jews nor Christians for your friends. They are friends with one another. Whoever of you seeks their friendship shall become one of their numbers. God does not guide wrongdoers. (S. 5:51)

This, the fifth sura, is the last of the revelations received by Mohammed just a few months before his death. In Arabic, "sura" means "a division or segment of Faith." In English it has a deeper meaning than just chapter.

Other passages strongly warn against trusting nonfollowers of the Prophet. Initially Jews and Christians had generated a widespread feeling of Arab spiritual inferiority because the Arabs had no prophet sent by God nor had they a special scripture of their own. Sadly, it was felt necessary because of past experiences of treachery, particularly by some Jewish tribesmen at the time of Mohammed's struggle against the leaders of his own tribe, the Quraysh. The Jews had made an alliance of support and friendship with Mohammed to defend monotheistic belief against the poly-theist Arab tribes. When Mohammed's few men were hopelessly outnumbered, the Jews turned and fought with the opposing tribes at the Battle of the Trenches in C.E. 627. The evil and vicious igno-miny of the Crusades for Christians is a later example of this. As Karen Armstrong indicates in her book *History of God,* prior to the Christian expulsion of the Muslims from Spain the Muslims made strong efforts to ensure that the relations between the communities of the three monotheistic faiths remained amicable. "The Muslims of Spain had given the Jews the best home they had had in the Di-aspora so the annihilation of Spanish Jewry was mourned by Jews, throughout the world as the greatest disaster to have befallen their people since the destruction of the Temple in C.E. 70."[1] It may be deduced that this betrayal was the reason for the above text and the continuing hostility and distrust between Jews, Christians, and Muslims into the twenty-first century.

However, later in the same sura it says: "Believers, Jews, Sabaeans and Christians—whoever believes in God and the Last Day and does what is right—shall have nothing to fear or regret" (S. 5:69). Among some disputed interpretations of the Koran is the sugges-tion that it foretells Jesus' return on the Day of Judgment and his defeat of the anti-Christ.

> Muslims have generally suggested that the defeat of Dajjal (the anti-Christ) will be in the hands of Isa (Jesus). Some es-chatological manuals go into lengthy detail describing the demise of the fallen angel Iblis (see S. 57:11-18) in this con-text, although there is no clarity in the understanding of Iblis' relationship to Dajjal.[2]

Suzanne Haneef, a convert to Islam who is active in the field of Islamic education writes, "Muslims hold that they themselves are much closer to the teaching of Jesus (God's peace and blessing be upon Him) than is the Christianity of the Church which they feel has been tampered with, and has distorted the Message which the Holy Messenger Jesus brought by ascribing divinity to himself."[3]

Haneef states that the major differences between the two faiths are the Doctrines of Original Sin and the Doctrines of the Godhead and the person of Christ. She says that these

> should not be taken as grounds for antagonism or heated theological arguments between Muslims and Christians. For what is common between followers of the two faiths is many basic beliefs and a vast legacy of moral injunctions and principles of behavior inspired by belief in the same God and the guidance conveyed by Jesus (Peace be on Him), which should inspire them in friendship, sympathy and appreciation for the other's sincerity, simply—"simply agree to disagree."[4]

Timidity in offering pastoral care to Muslims is not justified. My own experience has been one of mutual enrichment as I have ministered to Muslim patients. Times of fellowship in dialogue with Muslim leaders and other Muslims are remembered with fondness and thankfulness.

Mohammed, like the biblical prophets, had a distinctive role in turning people (Jews, Christians, and Arabs) from their idolatrous practices back to faith in the one, true, nonmaterial God of Abraham, Isaac, and Jacob. His zeal against idol worship had its effect on both Christianity and Judaism. Not much has been written on this aspect of the Prophet's ministry. Rabbis Maimonides (twelfth century C.E.) and Sholome (thirteenth century) both acknowledged Mohammed's contribution to faith and dependence upon God and not idols.

The following chapters will open some of the basic beliefs of the followers of Islam so that what may be argumentative points may be avoided.

Chapter 2

Muslims and God

The word "Islam" means "submission."

The word "Muslim" means "one who submits."

The followers of Islam are those who have submitted themselves to God. Submission, devotion, dedication, and a complete yielding to the will of God are the basic characteristics of a true Muslim believer. Unfortunately, as in all religions, including Christianity, a large proportion of those professing the faith are nominal and apathetic in their practice. These undermine the opportunity for others to gain a true impression of the merits of the religion.

THE ISLAMIC CREED

"There is no deity except God and Mohammed is the Messenger of God." From this simple statement of a Muslim's basic belief in the Oneness and Uniqueness of God and the Messengership of Mohammed stems all of Islam's concepts, attitudes, moral values and guidelines for human behavior.[1]

This simple yet basic creed makes extraordinary demands and places stringent obligations on the followers of God's message as given through Mohammed. One of the Hadith (traditions) formulated after the Prophet's death says:

Islam is based on five tenets:

1. The Testimony that there is no Deity except God and that Mohammed is his Servant and Messenger (The Kalima).

2. The Observance of Prayer (Salat).
3. The Giving of Alms (Zakat).
4. Fasting during Ramadan (Saum).
5. The Pilgrimage to Mecca (Hajj).

The Kalima is to be recited daily before others. It may be the simple minaret call to prayer (Adhan) or the creed. This daily confession stresses and reinforces the belief that God is one person and that through Mohammed's teaching this God is known and experienced.

Salat is a specific prayer formula, with arm raising, kneeling, and prostration. Salat fulfills a threefold purpose:

1. It acknowledges God's greatness.
2. It renews the covenant of submission.
3. It reminds the worshiper of the Day of Judgment.

Salat is offered five times per day at dawn, midday, midafternoon, sunset, and nightfall. Through this practice Muslims are seldom unaware of God and his requirements of them. Corporate prayers are offered at the Mosque on Friday.

> Believers, when you are summoned to Friday prayers hasten to the remembrance of God and cease your trading. That would be best for you, if you but knew it. Then when the prayers are ended, disperse and go your way in quest of God's bounty. Remember God always, so that you may prosper. (S. 62:9-10)

Saum (fasting) is practiced, particularly during Ramadan, the month when the first revelations were given to Mohammed. This suggests self-sacrifice and discipline, as food and drink are not to pass the gullet between sunrise and sunset for the whole month. The swallowing of saliva, which is already in the body, is permitted. The medical application of eye and ear drops do not nullify the fast. Persons ill or hospitalized are exempt from maintaining the full observance of the fast. During the fast abstinence from sexual intercourse is enjoined.

Believers, fasting is decreed for you as it was decreed for those before you; perchance you will guard yourselves against evil. Fast a certain number of days, but if any one among you is ill or on a journey, let them fast a similar number of days later; and for those who cannot endure it there is a ransom: the feeding of a poor man. He that does well of his own accord shall be well rewarded; but to fast is better for you, if you but knew it. (S. 2:183-184)

In the month of Ramadan . . . God desires your well-being, not your discomfort. He desires you to fast the whole month so that you may magnify Him and render thanks to Him for giving you guidance. . . . (S. 2:185)

Zakat (almsgiving) is the duty of every Muslim to provide for the poor. It is part of the practical application of the Islamic principles of the sharing of wealth and the equality of all. It is every Muslim's duty to account for personal property. The amounts of alms that are expected vary according to the different traditions. A common formula is one-fortieth of all assets (other than personal needs) per year and the feeding of one poor person per day.

A second issue of almsgiving is known as Fitr. This constitutes giving at the closing festival of Ramadan. Muslims of wealth must give alms of a day's food directly to poor Muslims for three consecutive days. Another aspect of this is that Muslims are forbidden to charge interest on loans to fellow Muslims.

The Hajj (pilgrimage) is to be made to Mecca at least once in a lifetime, if possible, according to wealth, health, and security.

Make a pilgrimage and visit the Sacred House for His sake. If you cannot, send such offerings as you can afford and do not shave your heads until the offerings reach their destination. But if any of you fall ill or suffers an ailment of the head, he must pay a ransom either by fasting or by almsgiving or by sacrifice. . . . Make the pilgrimage in the appointed months. He that intends to perform it in these months must abstain from sexual intercourse, obscene language, and acrimonious disputes while on pilgrimage. God is aware of what good you do. Provide well for yourselves: the best provision is piety. Fear Me, then, you that are endowed with understanding. (S. 2:196-197)

"WHAT IS GOD LIKE?"

The essence of Islam stems from opposition to the polytheistic worship of the Prophet's day. The return was to the concept of the monotheistic Abrahamic God who is one entity and not many. The opening words of the minaret call, "Allahu Akbar" (God the Almighty One)[2] is a strident declaration of this awesome God's authoritative power. Let the Koran describe this power.

> He is God, beside whom there is no other deity. He knows the unknown and the manifest. He is the Compassionate, the Merciful.
> He is God, beside whom there is other deity. He is the Sovereign Lord, the Holy One, the Giver of Peace, the Keeper of Faith; the Guardian, the Mighty One, the All-powerful, the Most High! Exalted be God above all idols!
> He is God, the Creator, the Originator, and The Modeller. His are the most gracious names. All that is in the Heavens and the earth give him the glory. He is the mighty, the Wise One. (S. 59:22-24)

> God; There is no god but Him, the Living, the Eternal One. Neither slumber nor sleep overtakes Him. He is what the heavens and the earth contain. Who can intercede with Him except by His permission? He knows what is before and behind men. They can grasp only that part of His knowledge which he wills. His throne is as vast as the heavens and the earth, and the preservation of both does not weary Him. He is the Exalted, the Immense One. (S. 2:255)

Haneef is critical of other religions describing their deities in anthropomorphic terms. Pictorial representations of God or the Prophet are strictly forbidden. Thirty or so years ago the *Times/Life* magazine had a depiction of the Prophet on its front cover. Authorities in both East and West Pakistan seized and destroyed all copies as being blasphemy. Professor Qamaruddin Khan informs us that the Koran tells us there is none other like God.[3] No human attributes are ascribed to God in order to avoid misunderstanding, false beliefs, and superstition. He uses procreation, citing Jesus (being called the Son of God) as an example of this blasphemy.

TAHWEED—THE UNITY OF GOD

Maudidi, a conservative and pragmatic Muslim scholar, encapsulates the essence of Islam when he writes, "The most fundamental and the most important teaching of the Prophet Mohammed (peace be upon Him) is faith in the Unity of God."[4] We have seen some of the Koran's descriptions of God, which are some of the most beautiful in all literature.

In the whole universe, Allah or God is the only one to be worshipped. Only to God is "Islam" (submission) and adoration to be made. He alone is Almighty. "He is concealed from our senses, and our intellect fails to perceive what He is," says Maudidi. This God is just so great a creator, controller, and governor of the universe that we cannot comprehend this awesome One. The Tahweed or Unity of God is the essential doctrine of Islam. Tahweed endeavors to explain how all these great attributes may be possessed without dissention, distortion, and corruption of the honor of this indescribable God. The primary Kalima (article of faith) already noted, short as it is, is for this reason to be repeated throughout each day. Thus this Unity of God is constantly being reinforced in the minds and consciousness of the believer.

"There is no deity but Allah [God]." By this belief in the unity and greatness of God a believer has a broad and universal outlook sensing the wonder of being part of the entire creation of God. In turn, the disciple sees everything else as belonging to God. Belief in this Kalima gives the Muslim courage and confidence in the face of life. Maudidi acknowledges two things that make men cowardly—the fear of death and the love of safety. Such fears arise because of a doubting belief. Is there someone else other than God who can influence life? The repeating of the Kalima purifies the mind of such fears.

Because all the believer's life and property belong to God, the believer willingly gives them up to God. The Kalima becomes the basis for and the stabilizing point for submission to be practiced. It is in God's time and God's action alone that our lives are directed.

UNITY VERSUS TRINITY

This belief in the Unity of God was fundamental to Mohammed's teaching. The received revelations provided an emphatic response to the polytheism of the majority of the Arab tribes of the Peninsular. Mohammed was on a mission of restoration of the old Abrahamic religion. As Haneef puts it,

> Islam does not claim to be a new religion. Rather it is the original religion, that primordial faith which has its roots deep in man's consciousness since the first true human being walked upon earth because the creator himself planted it there, the faith revealed and preached by all the prophets; the religion of submission and accountability to the one God.[5]

On reading the Koran one cannot but be struck by the influence of the Hebrew Old Testament upon the revelations. The patriarchs, kings, prophets of the Old Testament, and Jesus are repeatedly mentioned and quoted. However the fork in the road comes when Christians and the New Testament refer to Jesus as the divine "Son of God."

Followers of the Prophet call such a claim blasphemy. To ascribe to God the production of an avatar as the Gods of Hindu mythology seem able to give birth to is seen by them to be a repudiation of monotheism by Christians. Even today, Christians can offer them no satisfactory answers to their questions on the mystery of the Trinity. The nuances of Greek philosophical words will never satisfy the Islamic mind-set. We can say that Christianity appears to the Muslim to have taken the nonmonotheistic branch off the road of original religion.

The messages given to the Prophet acknowledge the divine source of the Hebrew Old Testament and the Gospel of Jesus.

Yet before it the Book of Moses was revealed: a guide and a blessing. This book confirms it. It is revealed in the Arabic tongue, to forewarn the wrongdoers and to give tidings to the righteous. (S. 46:12)

After them We sent forth Jesus, son of Mary, confirming the Torah already revealed, and gave him the Gospel, in which there is guidance and light, corroborating what was revealed before it in the Torah, a guide and admonition to the righteous. Therefore let those who follow the Gospel judge according to what God has revealed therein. Evil-doers are those that do not judge according to God's revelations. (S. 5:46-47)

He has revealed to you the Book with the Truth, confirming the scriptures which preceded it; for He has already revealed the Torah and the Gospel for the guidance of mankind, and the distinction between right and wrong.

Those that deny God's revelations shall be sternly punished; God is mighty and capable of revenge. Nothing on earth or in heaven is hidden from Him. It is He who shapes your bodies in your mothers' wombs as He pleases. There is no god but Him, the Mighty, the Wise One. (S. 3:3-4)

Jesus is believed to be the forerunner of Mohammed.

And of Jesus, son of Mary, who said to the Israelites: "I am sent forth to you from God to confirm the Torah already revealed and to give news of an apostle that will come after me whose name is Ahmad." Yet when he brought them clear signs, they say: "This is plain sorcery." (S. 61:6)

It is the claim of the divinity of Christ that is the stumbling block. Jesus is recognized as being in the line of prophets such as Elijah, Jeremiah, and Mohammed. The message of Jesus is a reemphasis upon obedience of the laws of God, submission to God, cleansing of the heart, and sincerity in worship of God instead of formalism in following ritual. Even the recognition of the virgin birth does not make Jesus divine. Sura 19 gives detail of Mary's annunciation and virgin conception of Jesus and even of Jesus talking from the cradle.

> Whereupon he spoke and said, "I am the servant of God. He has given me the Book and ordained me a prophet. His blessing is upon me wherever I go, and He has exhorted me to be steadfast in prayer and to give alms as long as I shall live. He has exhorted me to honour my mother and has purged me of vanity and wickedness. Blessed was I on the day I was born, and blessed shall I be on the day of my death and on the day I shall be raised to life."
> Such was Jesus, the son of Mary. That is the whole truth, which they still doubt. God forbid that He should Himself beget a son! When He decrees a thing He need only say: "Be," and it is. (S. 19:30-35)

The Koran repeatedly warns about accepting the concept of Jesus' divinity and even associating with Christians.

> People of the Book, [Christians] do not transgress the bounds of your religion. Speak nothing but the truth about God. Jesus, the Messiah, the Son of Mary was no more than a God's apostle and His word which he cast to Mary: a spirit from Him. So believe in God and his apostles and do not say: "Three." Forebear, and it shall be better for you. God is but one God. God forbid that He should have a son! His is all that the heavens and earth contain. God is the all-sufficient protector. The Messiah does not disdain to be a servant of God, nor do the angels nearest Him. Those who through arrogance disdain His service shall all be brought before Him. (S. 4:171-173)

> Unbelievers are those who say: "God is the Messiah, the son of Mary." For the Messiah himself said: "Children of Israel, serve God, my Lord and your Lord." He that worships other gods beside God, God will deny him Paradise, and the fire shall be his home. None shall help evil-doers.

Unbelievers are those that say: "God is one of three." There is but one God. If they do not desist from so saying, those of them that disbelieve shall be sternly punished." (S. 5:72-73)

The Jews say Ezra is the son of God, while the Christians say the Messiah is the son of God. Such are their assertions, by which they imitate the infidels of old. God confound them! How perverse they are!
They make of their clerics and their monks, and of the Messiah the Son of Mary, Lords beside God; though they were ordered to serve one God only. There is no god but Him. Exalted be He above those they deify beside Him! (S. 9:30-31)

Say: "People of the Book, let us come to an agreement: that we will worship none but God, that we will associate none with Him, and that none of us shall set up mortals as (deities beside God.)" (S. 3:65)

Say: God is one, the Eternal God. He begot none, nor was he begotten. None is equal to Him. (S. 112)

When conversing with hospital patients this is the one big hurdle that keeps many Muslims and Christians apart. When this issue is raised any fellowship between them disintegrates. The stance of both is equally offensive to the other. In the hospital context it is unwise to deal with this issue. A hospital patient is so concentrated on his or her illness and health that this type of theological discussion is too much and would be fruitless. A simple statement such as, "Christians believe that through the nature of his life and his teaching God is better understood" would be appropriate.

TAQWA—GOD CONSCIOUSNESS

Iman (faith in the creed) and taqwa are the essential requirements for being a good Muslim. As Haneef puts it, "Consciousness and fear of God are to govern all a Muslim's behavior; the acts of worship are a means to an end."[6] Taqwa has not an equivalent word in English. It signifies a special attitude toward God, which results in a distinct awareness of God and his will. Some endeavor to translate it as "God Consciousness." This conscious awareness of the indwelling presence of God brings the realization that God also is consciously aware of the worshipers' innermost thoughts and feelings. Haneef, in the previous quotation, high-lights "fear." She omits the other balancing element of taqwa—the intense love of the compassionate and merciful God, which is cru-cial to the relationship. Others have described taqwa as the mix-ture of fear and love that children have toward their father or teacher.

It is one of those cases in which we ask, "Which came first, the chicken or the egg?" Some would argue that the fear of God forces the believer to seek God and so love develops. Others would de-bate that out of the tremendous love for God there develops a fear of displeasing him by wrong thoughts, attitudes, and deeds. Both are vital characteristics to maintain the high sense of spiritual in-tensity, which is the earthly goal of the devout Muslim. Those who attain to such awareness are called Muttaqueen. Haneef's translation of the Koran uses the word:

> The Muttaqueen are those who spend (in God's way) in ease as well as in straitness, who restrain their anger and pardon men, for God loves those who do good; those who, when they commit an indecency or do injustice to their own souls, re-member God and ask for forgiveness for their sins—and who can forgive sins except God?—and do not knowingly persist in what they have done. For these the reward will be forgive-ness from their Lord and Gardens underneath which rivers flow, to abide therein, and (God's) favor, the reward of those who strive. (S. 3:134-136)[7]

The Muttaqueen are continually aware of the presence of God. This awareness affects all spiritual, moral and ethical behavior. It may be compared to the Christian concept of the "Fruits of the Spirit." It is readily possible to recognize a Muttaqueen by his or her serenity, saintliness, and graciousness.

The poor eighth-century Muslim slave woman Rabia fasted dur-ing the day while working and prayed most of the night, surviving on only short naps. Her master, noting her asceticism, devotion, and conscientious work, released her from her slavery. The follow-

ing prayer, attributed to her, indicates something of the depth of
the taqwa relationship with God.

> O, My Lord whatever share of this world you bestow upon
> me give it to your enemies; and whatever share of the next
> world you would give me, give it to your friends. You are
> enough for me.[8]

Read and reread this prayer. Reflect upon it. Venture to probe
the depth of Rabia's intimacy with God.

Muslim scholars suggest that it is a slow process to attain this
God consciousness. From childhood the existence, omnipresence,
the mercy of God, and personal responsibility and accountability
to God are to be spiritually ingested before the heights of taqwa are
gained.

For non-Muslims it is a privilege to come into the presence of a
muttaqueen. The aura of God's presence surrounds them, like that
exhibited by Christian mystics whose spirituality is highly developed and readily felt.

THE RIGHTS OF GOD

In these days when civil libertarians are airing their views on almost everything imaginable concerning human life, little is said
about the rights of God. Islam is aware of the rights the Absolute
One has in our lives. Maudidi's lofty reverence for God is alert to
God's rights in our lives. He identifies four rights God has over his
creation:

1. The right of God to demand that faith should be in him
   alone.
2. The right of God to demand wholehearted acceptance of his
   guidance.
3. The right of God to demand honest and unreserved obedience.
4. The right of God to demand full worship of him through
   prayers and submission.

Godly action and love follow belief. Belief in Islam leads to a life of action from within outward. Ansari describes belief as the root out of which shoots all human effort with its implications for morality and undivided loyalty to Allah, as well as a fear of the final accountability.[9] Thus the individual is able to proceed to a successful life. However, in practice it appears that this loyalty receives its impetus from fear.

Chapter 3

Fear and Hope

Primal religion sought to placate spirits, remedy social crises and personal trauma, cure illness, ensure good crops, produce healthy and good livestock, avert natural disasters, and so on. As religious thinking developed it sought to encourage acceptable behavior and perform austerities to attain an intimacy with the Divine. In time, work for a better status in the next life, the escape from reincarnation, entry into heavenly realms, and the attaining of reabsorption into Ultimate Reality, or the replacing of fear by a hope in the future dominated man's thinking. Humans, consistently throughout history, have been preoccupied with this fear of a future life or some form of what is or is not beyond death. Hindus and Buddhists fear a return to a lower animal form. Christians over the centuries have been hounded by fears of an eternity in the fires of hell. Muslims also have a dread of the Day of Judgment, when their status in the future life will be revealed.

In later chapters a look will be taken at some of their beliefs concerning, death, the intermediate state, and heaven and hell. Our immediate task is to identify the fear that stimulates the behavior of the Muslim, even to the crucial act of submission to God. In the Koran, two of the most basic truths revealed by the archangel Gabriel to Mohammed are the absolute oneness of God (tawhid) and the unavoidable coming of the judgment hour, when all humans will be accountable for their earthly behavior. The recognition of tawhid (the oneness and unity of God) is inevitably related to humans living a life of complete moral responsibility. Responsibility assumes that there will be a time of accountability.

Haneef writes,

> The Koran describes Hell (Gehenna) as a state of intense
> fearful burning and agony without respite, among the most
> horrifyingly loathsome surroundings and companions. But
> the awful part will be the terrible inescapable awareness that
> this is the destiny they deserved and brought upon themselves
> by rejecting God and ignoring the guidance, which he had
> conveyed through His Messengers.[1]

This reality of the future life is constantly before the consciousness of devout Muslims. As Haneef continues, "Yet no Muslim,
even the best of them, imagines that he is guaranteed Paradise; on
the contrary, the more conscious and God fearing one is, the more
he is aware of his own shortcomings and weaknesses."

From this it may be deduced that the Muslim must constantly
and sincerely seek to live according to God's decrees. It also may
be concluded that such striving increases, rather than diminishes,
fear of the future. Constant pressure is exerted to live up to the
standards, with any falter possibly proving to have negative results
for the future life. Knowledge of personal frailties may add to the
pressure.

Such an excessive fear gripped the Muslims in the early centuries following Mohammed's death. The Sufis began to moderate it
by centering on the inner self in contrast to external ritual. Sufism
became established and modified under the influence of Imam Al
Ghazali (C.E. 1058-1111). In 1096 he published four volumes con-
taining ten books. The third book of the fourth volume he titled
Fear and Hope.

Al Ghazali acknowledged the fearsome physical torments of
hell. He also described the spiritual torture of being separated
from earthly pleasures as well as being confronted by the deeds of
his own life. The crowning ignominy is in being denied entry into
the presence of God himself.

Islam teaches a middle ground. Al Ghazali in his book *Fear and
Hope* suggests that the fearsomeness of "The Day" is often portrayed in the Koran as when God talks to the Prophet:

Say! "Do but consider. Should this scourge fall upon you in the night or by the light of day, what punishment would the guilty hasten? Will you believe in it when it does overtake you, although it was your wish to hurry it on?"

Then will the wrongdoers be told: "Feel the everlasting torment! Shall you not be rewarded according to your deeds?"

They shall ask you if it is true. Say: "Yes, by the Lord, it is true! You shall not be immune." (S. 10:50-53)

Many are the texts that warn of the inevitability of being called to account for every deed and thought. Islam insists on a life after death to face such a day. The need for a personal accounting to God for our earthly sojourn is because each individual is different and unique. Our fingerprints, our DNA, our voices are uniquely ours. So are the deeds, emotions, and performances of our minds and spirits. There is not, among the many billions of humans who have existed, any two who are identical. Another person cannot match the totality of one's life's actions. Individual judgment, therefore, is inescapable and necessary.

Haneef quotes Hasn 'Izz al-Din Al-Jamal, who gives a space-age analogy:

Death is a missile which we ride to take us to this planet and this body we have is nothing but a space suit in which we appear on the stage of Life. . . . This game we play is measured to us and our motives are recorded intervals, they are short or long depending upon the length of our lives. Thus we ride death to return from whence we came to the house of decision, leaving behind us the costume or clothing which we call the body.[2]

Like Isaiah and Ezekiel, the Koran stresses this inescapability of Judgment:

The Hour of Doom is sure to come. But I choose to keep it hidden, so that every soul may be rewarded for its labors. Let those who disbelieve in it and yield to their desires not turn your thoughts from it, lest you perish." (S. 20:15)

Yet the unbelievers will never cease to doubt it until the Hour of Doom overtakes them unawares or the scourge of a baleful day descends upon them. On that day God will reign supreme. He will judge them all. Those that have embraced the true Faith and done good works shall enter the gardens of delight, but the unbelievers who have denied Our revelations shall receive an ignominious punishment. (S. 22:55-57)

"By the heaven with its starry highways, you contradict yourselves! None but the perverse turn away from the true faith. Perish the liars who dwell in darkness and are heedless of the life to come!

"When will the Day of Judgment be?" they ask. On that day they shall be scourged in the Fire, and a voice will say to them: "Taste this, the punishment that you have sought to hasten!" (S. 51:6-13)

Know that the life of this world is but a sport and a pastime, a show and an empty vaunt among you, a quest for greater riches and more children. It is like the plants that flourish after rain: the husbandman rejoices to see them grow; but then they wither away and turn yellow, soon becoming worthless stubble. In the life to come a grievous scourge awaits you—or the forgiveness of God and His pleasure. The life of this world is but a vain provision. (S. 57:20)

The Day of Judgment shall be horrific. Inhumanity shall be unprecedented in the frantic rush to escape its terror.

Therefore conduct yourself with becoming patience. They think the Day of Judgment is far off; but we see it near at hand.

On that day the sky will become like molten brass, and the mountains like tufts of wool scattered in the wind. Friends will meet, but shall not speak to one another. To redeem himself the sinner will gladly sacrifice his children, his wife, his brother, the kinsfolk who gave him shelter, and all the people of the earth, if then this might deliver him.

But the fire of Hell shall drag him down by the scalp, shall claim him who has turned his back on the true faith and amassed riches and covetously hoarded them. (S. 70:6-19)

Fisher concurs that Muslims believe that God's judgment is impartial. For the Muslim who fears the Day of Judgment and most do, some accept the teaching that believers will not have to endure Hell forever. Non-believers will remain there for eternity while others will be raised to Paradise.[3]

An Article of Faith in Islam is a belief in God's Decree, in other words, in what is ordained and planned by God. This decree has a positive and negative affect in relation to fear. Because the "All Powerful" is in control, the individual is released from fearing another human being or whatever else of boon or earthly disaster that may appear. The negative aspect of fear is that we must at all times be in fear of God because in his hands are the reins of control.

This fear is sustained in the minds of many by the belief in the doctrine of determinism, which we shall examine in the next chapter. If a balance is kept in reading the Koran then the believer should be filled with hope and faith in his or her caring and merciful God.

God alone is the source of blessing or harm to the believer and nonbeliever. Therefore the rigorous practice of the Five Pillars of Islam is with the primary motive of living lives that will be worthy and acceptable to God. Discipline in daily living is only achievable by constantly reminding oneself of who God is and what he expects of us. Obeying the Five Pillars of Islam ensures that spiritual blessings flow from personal desire and effort to achieve an intimacy with God through such exercises. Many who strictly observe the fulfillment of the Five Pillars of Islam could be asked if they would persist in the practices if the fear of the dire implications of the Day of Judgment were not so vivid. The Christian mystic, Thomas à Kempis, as did other mystics including Paul the Apostle, disciplined themselves in order to grow closer to God. It was James in his New Testament letter who spoke strongly about the conduct of the daily life by exercising faith with a matching work output.

For a number of weeks a patient with an incurable condition was in the hospital. After losing his business and property through the Beirut bombings he was now spending his last days suffering from cancer and its pain. Ali had much about which he could complain regarding the injustices of life. In my conversations and prayers with him every few sentences would be interrupted by the words, "Hum du'llah" meaning "praise be to God." For him to complain or dwell on those twinges of pain for which he uttered those words was, in his mind, tantamount to a complaint, even criticism, against God for his condition. To him, the Sovereign God had ordained his migration and cancer. The consequences for him if he showed dissent over God's Will for him would be Gehenna, not Paradise. Fear ruled. It was fear-induced action. The impressions of those daily contacts was Ali's fear of God's punishment if he showed the slightest intolerance of his condition, so he reacted by thanking and praising God for inflicting him with his cancer. He displayed a stoic acceptance of his painful and hopeless physical condition. To try to draw out of him his true mind toward his illness and flight from his homeland would have been spiritually destructive for him and an abuse of my rights to visit him and offer him support and care. Such action would have intensified his guilt and fear of God. Admirably, Ali was submitting himself to pleasing God, even on his deathbed.

It is considered that God created Gehenna to drive humans into the Garden. The thought is that insufficient fear produces softness toward moral responsibility, which leads to apathy and negligence of the spiritual imperatives. On the other hand, extreme fear causes depression, hopelessness, and despair. Both extremes cripple the development of a meaningful, positive relationship between the believer and God.

The first character of the Islamic personality is taqwa—God consciousness. As already mentioned, this comprises the love and fear of God—the greater the love, the greater the fear. This fear, with its consequential right living, is performed with the hope of attaining heavenly status. The saintly Rabia emphasized the love of God, which was uncontaminated by fear and hope of her eternal position. To quote Rabia again, "I have served him only for the love of him and desire for him."[4] Rabia exposes a purity of motive in her spirituality. All do not or are not able to attain to such heights of spiritual wisdom and experience. For the believer she displays a context for living in which fear does not dominate. Rabia almost overturns Al Ghazali's belief by evidencing that the greater the love the less the fear.

Islam in reality teaches a middle ground. Al Ghazali states "Fear and Hope are two wings by which flight is made to every commendable station." He adds, "Allah drives by the whip of fear and the reins of hope." He further speaks of "The whip of Fear curbed by the reins of Hope."[5] In Islam there is this balance. It may be said that fear is necessary in order to produce an appreciative hope. The faithful are enjoined to balance their fear of the future by embracing the hope that God to promises to those who submit to him. Here the word "submission" is paramount not only to belief but also applies to the practice of daily living, in all its aspects. Obedience to the call of submission should fill the true Muslim with a glorious hope.

For the Muslim, myriad Koranic verses present glowing pictures of Paradise and the Gardens. Paradise will be seen in more detail in Chapter 8 when we look at "the life beyond."

Before turning to the Koran for evidence of the hope that awaits the faithful, let us look at what Sufyan, who died in C.E. 777, as in McKane cited by Al Ghazali, said, "Whoever commits a sin and knows that God has assigned it against him, and (yet) hopes for His pardon God will pardon his sin."[6] The fear in Islam is the fear to fully submit to God and thereby sin against him. Sufyan is here saying that God will pardon such sin if we believe in the hope that he will. Sufyan appears dogmatic in his belief in this. This is not to say that this provides a license for us to sin. It then becomes like the insincere and abusive use of the Christian confession of faith many make. All Muslims are aware that God sees and knows our innermost secrets, motives, and thoughts. Fear of God through failure to submit to God is basic to Islam. The Koran warns those who fail to appreciate this,

> They use their faith as a disguise and debar others from the path of God. A shameful scourge awaits them.

> Their wealth and their children shall in no ways protect
> them from God. They are the inmates of the Fire, and there
> they shall abide for ever.
> On the day when God restores them all to life, they will
> swear to Him as they now swear to you, thinking that their
> oaths will help them. Surely they are all liars.
> Satan has gained possession of them and caused them to
> forget God's warning. They are confederates of Satan; they
> will surely be losers. (S. 58:16-19)

Paradise is also real. However, the warning is clear that the believer must retain that element of fear while anticipating a blessed
eternity.

> Believers, have fear of God and put your trust in His apostle.
> He will grant you a double share of his mercy, He will bestow
> upon you a light to walk in, and he will forgive you: God is
> forgiving and merciful. (S. 57:28-29)

Sura 70 speaks of the eternal situation describing the state of the
skeptic and the nonsubmissive on that day. Then it turns to believers.

> Not so worshippers who are steadfast in prayer; who set aside
> a due portion of their wealth for the beggar and the deprived;
> who truly believe in the Day of Reckoning, and dread the
> punishment of their Lord (for none is secure from the punish-
> ment of their Lord); who restrain their carnal desire (save
> with their wives and slave-girls, for these are lawful to them:
> he that lusts after other than these is a transgressor); who keep
> their trusts and promises and bear true witness; and who at-
> tend to their prayers with promptitude. These shall be laden
> with honors, in fair gardens. (S. 70:22-35)

Fair gardens, laden with honors—what a marvelous promise!
God will deal justly with all.

> We shall set up just scales on the Day of Resurrection, so that
> no man shall in the least be wronged. Actions as small as a

grain of mustard seed shall be weighed out. Our reckoning shall suffice.

We showed Moses and Aaron the distinction between right and wrong, and gave them a light and an admonition for righteous men: those who truly fear their Lord and dread the terrors of Judgement Day.

And in this (the Koran) we have revealed a blessed counsel. Will you then reject it? (S. 21:47-50)

The reward for true faithfulness is emphasized repeatedly.

Believers, Jews, Christians, and Sabaeans—whoever believes in God and the Last Day and does what is right—shall be rewarded by their Lord; they have nothing to fear or regret. (S. 2:62)

Surely the servants of God have nothing to fear or to regret. Those that have faith and keep from evil shall rejoice both in this world and in the hereafter: The word of God shall never change. That is the supreme triumph. (S. 10:64)

As for those that have faith and do good works, God will admit them to gardens watered by running streams. They shall be decked with pearls and bracelets of gold, and arrayed in garments of silk; they have been guided to the path of the Glorious Lord. (S. 22:22-23, cp. The Epistle of James)

But in fair gardens the righteous shall dwell in bliss, rejoicing in what their Lord will give them. Their Lord will shield them from the scourge of Hell. He will say: Eat and drink to your hearts content. This is the reward for your labors.

They shall recline on couches arranged in rows. To dark eyed houris We shall wed them.

(We shall unite the true believers with those of their descendants who follow them in their faith, and shall not deny them the reward of their good works; each man is the hostage of his own deeds.)

Fruits We shall give them, and such meats as they desire. They will pass from hand to hand a cup inspiring no idle talk, no sinful urge; and there shall wait upon them young boys of their own, as fair as virgin pearls. (S. 52:15-24)

Therefore strive for the pardon of your Lord, and for a Paradise as vast as heaven and earth, prepared for those who believe in God and His apostles. Such is the grace of God: He bestows it on whom He will. God's grace is infinite. (S. 57:21)

The fear of not being fully submissive is an acknowledgement of God's sovereignty and puts the mind of the Muslim in pursuit of a greater knowledge of God and his desires for daily living. Every new insight into the nature of God reveals him to be more than a fearful judge. This God is a merciful and pardoning God who at the same time is able to elicit from us a growing love for him. By this confidence is gained an assurance of His willingness to forgive personal sin. Such forgiveness puts us into a hopeful relationship with Him so that our anticipation of a place in the gardens of Paradise becomes a realistic hope.

The Muslim hospital patient needs to be reminded that the fruits of obedience and submission to God are forgiveness and a solid and firm hope for a "Holy" life beyond the grave. The faith factor is strong in practical Islam, therefore Muslim believers should be encouraged in their faith.

Chapter 4

Determinism and Free Will

Among the Arab tribes in pre-Islamic times, the understanding of the Godhead was that he created the world and humankind and then left his creation to its own devices. There was nothing but this present world. We live and die with nothing destroying us but time. Although a few Arabs still believed in the monotheistic God of Abraham, the remainder worshipped a multiplicity of gods or spirits. Some reports are that at the time of the restoration of the Kabaah in Mecca where the great Mosque was established there were 360 idols removed. The Koran brought drastic change, placing humans in the hands of a just, compassionate, merciful God, who declared that death was not the end but the passage into a new eternal existence.

If this is the case, it must be asked of our hospital patient Ali from Beirut, "How can you uphold your remarkable degree of stoicism, courage, acceptance, and patience in the face of your suffering?" It was suggested that it was a fear of God and of his own future status in this eternal life.

Perhaps his understanding of the Koran and the Hadith were dominating his mind.

> Say: "Nothing will befall us except what God has ordained. He is our Guardian. In God let the faithful put their trust." (S. 9: 51)

> "It is he who created you from clay. He has decreed a term for you in this world and another in the next. Yet you are still in doubt. He is God in the heavens and on earth. He has knowledge of all that you hide and all that you reveal. He knows what you do." (S. 6:2-3)

"Every misfortune that befalls the earth, or on your own persons, is ordained before we bring it into being. That is easy enough for God; so that you may not grieve for the good things you miss, or be overjoyed at what you gain. God does not love the haughty, the vainglorious; nor those who, being niggardly themselves, enjoin others to be niggardly also. He that gives no heed should know that God alone is self-sufficient and worthy of praise." (S. 57:22-24)

Ali would have been made aware of these scriptures from early childhood. It is the responsibility of the parents to instruct their children in the Muslim way. When the age of puberty is reached a child should be well grounded in the fundamentals of the faith. This doctrine of determinism or predestination of necessity is taught as essential to the role of God as the Sovereign Lord.

The traditions emphasize determinism. It may also be called fatalism. An embryo's sex, sustenance, date of death, and eternal destiny are decreed within the first forty days of conception.[1]

Modern acceptance of fatalism leads some Muslims to refuse to take medicine, as this may interfere with God's plan. Some traditions also go so far as to assert that Adam ate the fruit because God willed it.

This doctrine has caused much controversy within Islam as well as amongst some observers of Islam. The predetermination of a person's life and history has so dominated Islamic theology that it has permeated every strata of society. The educated and affluent, the ill-educated and poor have a firmly entrenched belief that whatever a person does, says, thinks, or befalls in life occurs directly as willed by God.

Some schools of Judeo-Christian thought of the early Christian centuries complemented this teaching. Both Judaism and Christianity have deflated the influence of predestination ideas in recent centuries. Calvinistic and Reformed traditions still foster this absolute sovereign authority of God over all the big as well as the insignificant happenings on the earth. It is not uncommon to hear practicing and nonpracticing Christians say, "When my time is up, it is up"; "When your number comes up there is nothing you can do about it"; or after a survival from death, "It wasn't my time." This is a similar type of determinism or fatalism as is found Islam.

Raphael Patai, in his book *The Arab Mind,* writes, "God is said to determine the character of each person. Neither the individual himself, nor the external factors, can change a man's God given character, which remains with him throughout his life and which destines him for a certain way of life."[2] Patai refers to Hilma Granqvist, who reported that the villagers of Artas outside Bethlehem believed that man has no other option but to conform to every detail of God's decree for his life. Edward Lane's observations in Cairo were similar. He quotes a special prayer said annually on the fifteenth of the month of Sha'ban, when God believed to reconfirm the predetermined events for each individual for the ensuing year. The following is part of that prayer:

> O God, O Thou gracious . . . If you, have recorded me in thy abode, upon the "Original of the Books," miserable or unfortunate, or scanted my substance, cancel, O God, of thy goodness, my misery, and misfortune and scanty allowance of substance, and confirm me in thy abode upon the "Original of the Books" as happy and provided for, and directed to good. . . .[3]

This prayer affirms the belief that all is preordained. It assures God that the believer so praying is happy at the provision God has willed and that he knows it will be for his own ultimate good. Surely this was the faith Ali was exhibiting on his deathbed.

The Koran stresses the inevitability of events and no one, not even other objects or persons of worship, can change it.

> The blessings God bestows on men none can withhold; and what He withholds none can bestow, apart from Him. He is the Mighty, the Wise One. (S. 35:2)

This is echoed in the words of Jesus speaking before Pilate:

> You would have no authority at all over me, if it had not been granted you from above. (John 19:11 *REB*)

> Every misfortune that befalls the earth, or your own person, is ordained before We bring it into being. That is easy enough for God: so that you may not grieve for the good things you miss, or be overjoyed at what you gain. (S. 57:22)

The Hadith support it. Haneef quotes, "God has predestined everything in a person's life. Any attempt to change or alter those predeterminations would be in vain. Any such attempt would be to ascribe powers to another which God alone possesses."[4]

What then should be the attitude of the Islamic believer? It would be easy to adopt a fatalistic stance, in which one just sits and apathetically waits for events to unfold.

Haneef continues, "Islam teaches, the task of the human being is to sincere effort to strive to do his best." As Haneef points out, the person cannot know beforehand what is to happen or how it will turn out. Therefore the responsibility is to perform in any situation to the best of one's ability to attain the best possible result. God's predetermined plan is not complete until such effort has been made. This raises questions, such as if the person does not put in his or her best effort, how can God's pre-ordained result be accomplished? This is but one of the problems such a rigid deterministic belief raises. It also may be asked, "If God has inflexibly predestined a person's life, why is there then a need for a Day of Judgment and Accounting?"

Can it be deduced from the Koran that judgment will be determined on the basis of our acceptance of our complaint against the events predestined for us? Ali's repetition of "Hum du'llah"—"Praise be to God"—seems to confirm his belief that this was so. Praise for the ravages of war, his cancer, and his pain seem incongruous to the non-Muslim. Yet to the Muslim it is a clear indication of the person's patience, grace, trust in, dependence upon, and total submission to God. It echoes the Christian Paul in his letter to the Church at Philippi:

> I have learned to be satisfied with what I have. I know what it is to be in need and what it is to have more than enough. I have learned this secret, so that anywhere, at any time, I am content, whether I am full or hungry, whether I have too much

or too little. I have strength to face all conditions by the power that Christ gives me. (Philippians 4:11-13 *GNB*)

Paul was fully dedicated and submissive to the Divine Will. Paul's statement is a prime example of the grace, which God bestows on those who are willing to submit themselves into his guidance, love, and care.

Let us look at the three expressions that are frequently uttered by Muslims in an effort to safeguard their place in God's plan for their eternal future. These indicate how deeply determinism is ingrained into the mind.

"Bishmi'llah" (in the name of God) is uttered whenever a Muslim tells anything, hears anything, does anything, or receives news.

"Hum du'llah" (thanks be to God) is repeated when anything good or evil befalls the Muslim, as in the patient Ali's case.

"Inshallah" (if God wills) is used when referring to anything that may happen in the future. Determinism in Islam denudes the Muslim of any thought, concern, or talk of plans and action unless covered by the utterance of "inshallah." Many Christians may say something like; "I plan to do that next week—God willing." For the Muslim "inshallah" has a deeper and more significant meaning as it relates to the desire not to displease God or appear critical of his decrees for the person's life.

A Muslim boy had been struck by a car and was in the pediatric intensive care unit. The mother was grief stricken. On her return to the unit the next morning after attending to the other members of the family, her body showed massive bruising. She had battered her body in her display of grief over her son's condition. The Koran forbids the mutilation of the human body as God's creation. In practice, Islam tolerates such grief reactions. Among village people of all religions, magic and superstitions have been practiced for centuries, often contrary to their theological position. The superstitious observances of the religious Irish, Spanish, French, Portuguese, and Italian villagers are no less contradictory than those of the Muslim villagers who see the "eye" as the dispenser of evil and not God.

A coin always has two sides. Christianity has struggled in controversy over predestination and election. The Antithesis has always been evident in the foreground—free will. Islam, like Christianity, still is embroiled in the same debate—God's will versus free will.

The question of a human exercising his or her free will to determine a course of action in any given situation appears to override God's sovereignty. Some Christians and many Muslims see, in free will, the abrogating of the powers of God. It is seen to be the setting up of humans alongside of God.

Can and does free will claim a right, from the Koran, to be seriously considered?

Some passages of the Koran point to free will. It was declared a heresy in C.E. 715, some eighty years after Mohammed. One of the reasons propounded was that it set up the individual as a co-creator with God, able to determine his or her own actions and destiny. Among Islamic leaders of the time it was considered to have its origins in Christianity. We must recognize the dominating effect determinism/fatalism has upon the minds of Muslims. However "Divine Sovereignty" and "Human Responsibility" are complementary ideas in the Koran.

Some schools of thought in Islam cannot accept that God wills and is responsible for all the evil that happens in the world. Patai is not surprised that predestination is accepted on one "level of consciousness" while actual behavior belies it.[5]

In many Muslim-majority countries, when strolling through the bazaars and shops or looking at ornaments on clothing, one will often see a swatch of blue. Others may wear a brooch fashioned with a blue eye in the center of the hand of Fatima (Mohammed's daughter). Simple villagers follow traditional practices to deter the influence of the evil eye. Blue is considered the magical color that the eye avoids. Beloved male children may be dressed unkempt in soiled girl's dresses until age five years to dupe the evil eye into thinking he is an unappealing girl. A baby's eye may be heavily underlined with mascara for a similar reason. There are many magical practices performed for realizing a wish, healing an ailment, casting a spell, and so on. Patai identifies the origins of these as from pre-Islamic times. Official Islam disapproves of such practices, yet tolerates them—justifying the ignoring of them because the practitioners believe in God and his Prophet alone.

In raising this duality the question must be asked, "If God is sovereign, does determinism extend to non-Muslims? This parallels with the Christian controversy of election. God elected to save some and decreed the rest to be eternally damned. The Islamic doctrine of predestination would also give the impression that if God has ordained a person's total history in the first forty days after conception then some are destined for Gehenna before they are born. Surely this arbitrary playing with human lives does not tally with the merciful and compassionate God of the Koran.

The question of absolute predeterminism is called into question within the Koran itself. God does not guide everyone, and certainly not evildoers.

> How will God guide those who lapse into unbelief after embracing the Faith and acknowledging the Apostle as true, after receiving veritable proofs? God does not guide evildoers. Their reward will be the curse of God, the angels, and all mankind; under it they shall abide for ever. Their punishment shall be reprieved; except those that afterward repent and mend their ways, for God is forgiving and merciful.
>
> But those that recant after accepting the true faith and grow in unbelief, their repentance shall not be accepted. These are the truly erring ones. (S. 3:86-90)

If God does not guide evildoers, then God is not responsible for the evil about us. By not guiding evildoers there is the admission that God is not in control of such persons' lives. Here it must be conceded that humans have the ability to choose faith or evil. In the same sura, v. 103, God urges fear of himself and to cling to the faith, not allowing anything to separate them from him. There, then, must be the opportunity for freedom to choose to follow or reject.

The modernist Islamic writers and theologians are more outspoken emphasizing accountability as affirming "individuality and individual free will." Some take an extreme Islamic position by advocating "God in His Absolute Wisdom has given man complete freedom."[6] This does not seem to accord with what we have already stated. The question of human responsibility provides a dilemma that is contrary to God's absolute sovereignty; humans have a measure of freedom to make decisions concerning their own lives and actions. In Sura 2 Adam followed Satan's word and not God's. Here is the first man making a decision of personal choice. When Adam repented and God forgave him, God said:

> When My guidance is revealed to you, those that accept My Guidance shall have nothing to fear or to regret; but those that deny and reject Our revelations shall be the inmates of the Fire, and there they shall abide for ever. (S. 2:38-39)

Here is a clear statement that humans will be able to accept or reject God's guidance. In speaking of humans the angel said:

> He created man from a little germ: yet he is openly contentious [an open opponent]. . . . God alone points to the right path. Some turn aside but had he pleased he would have given you guidance all. (S. 16:4 and 9)

It almost seems a contradiction. In verse 4 man is an opponent of God and therefore it must be argued that some men are rebellious and do not respect or obey God's word—in other words exercise free will. Verse 9 indicates that God directs only those whom He wills down the right path. This seems to indicate no free choice.

The Koran speaks frequently of humans' ingratitude to God, which it must be assumed is seen in our disobedience or the use of free will.

> . . . man is ungrateful to His Lord! To this he shall bear witness. (S. 100:6-7)

> We have endowed him with sight and hearing and, be he thankful or oblivious of our favors, We have shown him the right path. (S. 76:3)

Ingratitude is characteristic of some humans. It is perceived that God would be displeased in humans making choices for themselves that ran contrary to his purposes. Sura 96 speaks of humans transgressing by thinking of themselves as being their own masters. This all amounts to humans making thier own choices.

The way humans are described by Haneef is more forthright.

> For man, Islam asserts, is a unique creation of God's, possessing an obvious outward aspect—a physical body—and a hidden inner aspect—the mind, emotions, and soul. The uniqueness of man's nature lies in the fact that he has been endowed with freedom of choice, judgment between right and wrong, capacities for thinking, transmitting knowledge, feeling and acting. These have not been given to other creatures, nor have they an immortal soul which lives on after the death of the physical body.[7]

She has no doubts of God's gift to humans of a free will. She considers that this enables humans to willingly and deliberately make a choice to be guided by God. By such a choice humans are able to avoid following their own chaotic impulses, desires, and fancies. Following such advice enables us to act responsibly.

Because God has absolute wisdom and knowledge, by a voluntary submitting of oneself to God and his guidance, one is assured of the best of both the present and the future worlds. Our greatest choice, according to Haneef, is to decide who is the Lord of our lives and worship—human ideas and desires or God the Compassionate and Merciful.

Where does determinism fit in with this idea of our freedom to choose God as Lord? Many may feel they are able to make choices including that of submitting to God and still to be in control of their own affairs. The Koran speaks of God's creativeness in the beginning and of his knowledge of the past, present, and the future and that whatever humans decide God is in control and that in the end all must return to him for judgment.

Despite our ability to make decisions, we are dependent upon Him for existence and sustenance. As Haneef suggests, humans may strive to choose, will, and act to their utmost best but it is God who decides the result of those best efforts. It appears that Haneef is suggesting that although there is freedom to decide, we are best advised to submit to God and let him guide and direct our lives.

We shall be tried and tempted by good and evil. God will put us to the test even as we live exercising our free will.

> Every soul shall taste of death. We will prove you all with evil and good. To Us you shall return." (S. 21:35)

> Do men think that once they say: "We are believers," they will be left alone and not be put to the test? We tested those who have gone before them. God surely knows those who are truthful, as he assuredly knows the liars.
> Or do evildoers think they will escape Our reach? How ill they judge! (S. 29:1-4)

> We shall test your steadfastness with fear and famine, with loss of property and life and crops. Give good news to those who endure with fortitude; who in adversity say: "We belong to God, and to Him we shall return." On such men will be God's blessing and mercy; such men are rightly guided. (S. 2:155-157)

> God does not change people's lot unless they change what is in their hearts. If God seeks to inflict them with misfortune, none can ward it off. Besides Him, they have no protector.
> It is He who makes the lightning to flash upon you, inspiring you with fear and hope, as He gathers up the heavy clouds.
> The Thunder sounds His praises, and the angels, too, for awe of Him. He hurls His thunderbolts at whom He pleases. Yet unbelievers wrangle about God. Stern is His might. (S. 13:12-13)

By such testing God is able to make us aware of good and evil, right and wrong, and thereby enable us to conform to or be submissive to his ways. It is particularly for those who abrogate to themselves the ability to choose. God is always there and through this testing is seeking to guide us along the true path. Through such trial we are forced to remember God. Remembrance of God is important.

The conservative Muslim scholar Maudidi declared that there is free will.[9] Free will is to choose Islam or kufr (rejection of god). He might have included the other two unpardonable sins: (1) shirk (failure to accept the teachings of the Prophet, infidelity to the faith); and (2) murder. The natural thing to do is to obey God. God, in giving the ability to gain knowledge and reason, gave this freedom of will and action to be tested.

The danger in stretching the free will concept is that man will follow egotistical desires rather than submitting to God. Various Muslim magazines constantly publish articles warning Muslim young people from being trapped into the ways of the decadent Western permissive society where morals and ethics are almost forgotten. These articles have a sound observable basis. Modern Western society has allowed free will to be exercised without bridle.

If Haneef's argument is correctly interpreted then humans are free to choose, to will, and to act. God determines the result of all that freedom. True freedom is not found in the abandonment of rules and controls. It was Jesus, The Christ, who said, "You will know the truth, and the truth will set you free" (John 8:32 *REB*). For the Muslim as well as for the Christian, truth is found in full submission to God and God's will. In so doing true freedom is found.

Is this the ground where determinism and free will meet? Freedom to choose the way of submission. By following this choice God guides the Muslim into eternal blessing.

Chapter 5

Iblis, Angels, and Jinn

To understand the thinking of hospitalized Muslims it is necessary to know something of their expectations of the future and the participants who are involved in their progress to the hereafter. The same requirements are necessary in meeting Christians, Hindus, Buddhists, and others in a similar setting.

Zoroastrianism, the strongly developing religion in the days of the Jewish exile under Nebuchadnezzar, influenced Judaism's, Islam's, and Christianity's understanding of death and eschatological events. Zoroastrianism highlighted angels, demons, and other celestial beings as well as depicting grotesque eschatological figures such as may be seen in the New Testament book of Revelation. Post-exilic Jewish literature exhibits its influence.

Zoroastrians believe, like all the three major monotheistic religions, that each of us will be judged according to our deeds—good and bad. They believe that they will have to cross the "Bridge of Chinvat"—The Bridge of Judgment—to heaven—the "Kingdom of Right." This is where the righteous will abide. The bridge narrows according the accumulated evil of the deceased. For the utterly sinful, the bridge will be so narrow that they will not be able to cross over. From there they will fall off the bridge into hell—"The House of the Lie." Reference to this will be made later. The evil spirits possess the dead bodies minus the soul—"The Tower of Silence" for the bodies to be defleshed by vultures.

The founder Zarathustra, called by Greeks Zoroaster, diversely reported as living somewhere between 1200 and 500 B.C.E. Some scholars even place him as living 9500 B.C.E. He is considered to be the first of all the monotheists in Western tradition. Ahura Mazda is the Supreme, eternal creator of all good things, the All

Wise and Lord of Life and Truth. From this Godhead emerged six attributes:

1. The good mind
2. Order, eternal truth, and righteousness
3. Absolute power
4. Devotion
5. Perfection
6. Immortality

He also expounded the teaching of two great opposing forces—Spenta Mainyu, the good spirit, and Angra Mainyu, the evil spirit. The lattter is described as nonlife, imperfection, chaos, disease, sorrow, and destruction. Zoroastrians must dedicate themselves to the good spirit.[1] This struggle between the forces of good and evil expanded. Thus angels, demons, the end of the world, a final judgment, the resurrection, and heaven and hell were adopted in varying forms into these other religions.

Farnaz Ma'sumian writes, "Zoroaster was probably the first prophet in history to speak of a universal judgment at death." The Gathas (one of the earlier scriptures) describe the fate of the souls after death. They depict Paradise as the best postdeath place. The state of the souls is described:

> Their own soul and their own self will torment them when they come to the "Bridge of the Separator." To all time will they be guests of the "House of the Lie." (Yasna 46:11)

Here the soul will suffer alone forever.

Later texts describe the evil demon "Vizaresha" dragging the wicked onto the bridge. There is a triad of heavenly judges (Mithra and his aides Sraosha and Rashnu). Nonhumans opposing good and evil spirits are a significant part of Zoroastrian teaching.

Islam believes in nonhuman beings created by God including Iblis, jinn, and angels. It is popularly conceived that Iblis is the equivalent of Satan. The angels are God's supporters for good and Iblis and the jinn are the forces of evil.

IBLIS (SATAN)

The longest Sura of the Koran is Sura 2 (Al-Baqara—The Cow). The prophet is reported to have claimed that this chapter is the "pinnacle" of the Koran. It deals with the most important doctrines of the faith. In contains the story of the creation of Adam as the pride of creation. God orders all other created intelligent beings to bow down to Adam. Iblis refuses to do so. From this the fall of man is directly attributed to Satan.

> And when We said to the angels: "Prostrate yourselves before Adam," they all prostrated themselves before Adam except Satan, who in his pride refused and became an unbeliever . . .
>
> But Satan removed them thence and brought about their banishment. "Get you down," We said, "and be enemies of each other. The earth will provide your dwelling and your sustenance." (S. 2:34, 36)

The story is developed in Sura 7:

> Then We said to the angels: "Prostrate yourselves before Adam." They all prostrated themselves except Satan, who refused to prostrate himself.
>
> "Why did you not prostrate yourself when I commanded you?" He asked.
>
> "I am nobler than he," he relied. "You created me from fire, but you created him from clay."
>
> He said, "Get you down hence! This is no place for your contemptuous pride. Away with you! Henceforth you shall be humble."
>
> He replied: "Reprieve me till the Day of Resurrection."
>
> "You are reprieved." He said.
>
> "Because you have led me into sin," he [Satan] declared, "I will waylay your servants as they walk on Your straight path, then spring upon them from the front and the rear, from the right and the left. Then you will find the greater part of them ungrateful."

"Begone!" He said. "A despicable outcast you shall hence-
forth be.' As for those that follow you, I shall fill Hell with
you all." (S. 7:11-18)

Sura 15 adds to the narrative.

He [Iblis] replied, "I will not bow to a mortal whom you created out of dry clay, of black mounded loam."
     "Begone," said God, "you are accursed. My curse shall be
upon you till Judgment Day.". . .
     "Lord," said Satan, "since you have seduced (sent me
astray) me, I will tempt mankind on earth: I will seduce them
all, except those who are your faithful servants."
     He [God] replied, "This is My Straight Path. You shall
have no power over My servants, only the sinners who follow
you. They are all destined for hell."   (S. 15:33-35, 39-43)

Suras 17, 18, and 38 repeat the story of Iblis's disobedience.
Iblis's fate on the Day of Judgment is to be cast into the fires of
Hell with all the unbelievers and those he led astray.

And into Hell shall they be hurled, they and those that misled
them, and Satan's legions all. "By the Lord," they will say to
their idols, as they contend with them, "we erred when we
made you equals with the Lord of the Universe. The evil-doers
led us astray. We have no intercessors now, no loving friend.
Could we but live our lives again we would be true believers."
(S. 26:95-98)

On the Day of Judgment Iblis, the fallen angel, will be over-
come by the Mahdi (the Savior). More will be said of the Madhi
later. Iblis's destruction and casting into the fires is the first stage
of the drama of the Hour of Doom.

ANGELS

Many religions have beliefs of a hierarchy of celestial beings that
assist God/the gods. The four religions mentioned have a strong belief in angels as delineated in their sacred scriptures. The activities

of angels are more prominent in Islam than in Judaism or Christianity. They are credited with the responsibility of relaying God's messages to humankind. Among the basic tenets of Islam is the belief in angels along with God, the scriptures, and the prophets.

> The Apostle believes in what has been revealed to him by his Lord, and so do the faithful. They all believe in God, His Angels, His scriptures, and His apostles: We discriminate against none of his apostles. (S. 2:285)

> Praise be to God, Creator of the heavens and the earth! He sends forth the angels as His messengers, with two, three or four pair of wings. He multiplies His creatures according to His will. God has power over all things. (S. 35:1)

> By His will He sends down angels with the Spirit to those among His servants whom he chooses, bidding them proclaim: "There is no god but Me: therefore fear Me." (S. 16:2)

It was God's angelic messenger, Gabriel, who delivered God's revelation to the Prophet. These revelations cemented this strong belief. Angels such as Gabriel are nonphysical beings created by God to serve and worship him. Angels exist in large numbers and have special responsibilities. The Koran tells us that angels are continually observing all our actions. These angels are completely subservient to God. In this they differ from Iblis.

God informed the angels of his decision to create humans and place them upon the earth. These angels questioned God about it. They were concerned that humans might do harm on earth and kill what is on the earth.

> When your Lord said to the angels: "I am placing on the earth one that shall rule as My deputy," they replied, "Will You put there one who will do evil and shed blood, when we have for so long sung Your praises and sanctified Your name?" (S. 2:30)

Angels had prior knowledge of God's proposed actions even delivering details to them. Being God's messengers, they had to relay and implement God's word to humans. The angels came to Zacha-

riah, the father of John the Baptist, as well as coming to other believers and unbelievers.

> As he [Zacharias] stood praying in the Shrine, the angels
> called out to him saying, "God bids you rejoice in the birth of
> John, who shall confirm the Word of God. He shall be princely
> and chaste, a prophet and a righteous man." (S. 3:38-39)

> Believers, guard yourselves and guard yo ur kindred against
> a Fire fueled with men and stones, in charge of fierce and
> mighty angels who never disobey God's command and who
> promptly do His bidding. They will say to unbelievers: "Make
> no excuses for yourselves this day. You shall be rewarded ac-
> cording to your deeds." (S. 66:6)

A significant role for angels is as guardians of the believers and
they are not to be worshipped. This contrasts with the responsibility of delivering the unfaithful souls to God for Judgment and the
reference to the angel of death.

> No mortal to whom God has given the scriptures and whom
> He has endowed with judgment and of prophethood would
> say to men: "Worship me instead of God." But rather: "Be de-
> voted servants of God, for you have studied and taught the
> Scriptures." Nor would he enjoin you to serve the angels and
> the prophets as your gods; for would he enjoin you to be un-
> believers after you have surrendered yourselves to God?
> (S. 3:79-80)

> As for those who say: "Our Lord is God," and take the
> straight path to Him, the angels will descend to them, saying,
> "Let nothing alarm you or grieve you. Rejoice in the Paradise
> you have been promised. We are your guardians in this world
> and the hereafter. There you shall find all that your souls de-
> sire and all that you can ask for: a rich provision from a for-
> giving and merciful God." (S. 41:30-32)

> He reigns supreme over His servants. He sends forth guard-
> ians who watch over you and carry away your souls without

fail when death overtakes you. Then are all men restored to
their true Lord. His is the Judgment and most swift is His
reckoning. (S. 6:61-62)

What will they do when the angels carry off their souls,
striking their faces and their backs?
That is because they follow what has incurred the wrath of
God and abhor what pleases Him. He will surely bring their
works to nothing. (S. 47:27-28)

Say: "The angel of death in charge of you will reclaim your
souls. Then to your Lord you shall return." (S. 32:11)

This angelic role of being God's messengers has many aspects.
They must steer men along the straight path, be their guardians,
and deliver them from the fate of the unbelievers. The only seemingly contradictory role is that of being the recorders of every
person's every action for presentation on the Day of Judgment. It
is upon these records that the person's status in hell or paradise is
determined. The belief is that every person has two recording angels observing him or her all the time. "Surely there are guardians
watching over you, noble recorders who know of your actions"
(S. 82:9-10)

Because of the supreme glory, awesomeness, and magnificence
of God, humans are unable to approach him in his human state.
God in his wisdom has selected prophets to make his mind known
to the people through the agency of angels. Angels are the commu-
nicators for God to his creation.

JINN

There are also other beings. They include jinn (jinnee). Jinn are
separate creations of God and, now, try to lead people astray.
Haneef refers to jinn as "another species of intelligent beings" and,
in a footnote claims, "According to Islam, Satan (Iblis or Shayten)
and his kind are jinn (not fallen angels) to whom God gave leave to
try and tempt man, to lure him away from submission and obedience to Him. . . . The Qu'ran makes it clear that one whose life is

centered on God can easily repel Satan, whose strategy is weak. . . ."3
She, also, states that jinn do not have a free will like men. Others
see jinn as having also the ability to promote good and have a role
differing from Satan.

> The Blaspheming One [Iblis] among us has uttered a wanton
> falsehood against God, although we had supposed that no
> man or jinnee could tell of God what is untrue.
> (Some men have sought the help of jinn, but they misled
> them into further error. Like you they thought that God could
> not resurrect the dead.) (S. 72:4-5)

> Mankind and jinn, we shall surely find the time to judge
> you! Which of your Lord's blessings would you deny?
> Mankind and jinn, if you have the power to penetrate the
> confines of heaven and earth, then penetrate them! But this
> you shall not do except with Our own authority. Which of
> your Lord's blessing would you deny? (S. 55:33-34)

> We have predestined for hell numerous jinn and men. They
> have hearts that they cannot comprehend with; they have eyes
> they cannot see with; and they have ears they cannot hear
> with. They are like beasts—indeed, they are more misguided.
> Such are the heedless. (S. 7:180-181)

Non-Muslims are accused, in the Koran, of suggesting that God
produced sons and daughters and that the angels were daughters.
The revelations continue:

> They assert kinship between Him and the jinn. But the jinn
> well know that they will all be called to account. Exalted be
> God above their imputations. (S. 37:16)

Sura 6 highlights the Oneness and Unity of God, proving his su-
premacy in dealing with men and the earth around them. Rafiq
Zakaria, in his commentary on this Sura, says, "Through the story
of Abraham, who disowned his father to prove his loyalty to his
Lord, virtues of religious fidelity are emphasized."4 Here is reference to Abraham's separation from his polytheistic family, object-

ing to their ascribing associates alongside of God. Here Gabriel speaks of these nonbelievers:

> Yet they regard jinn as God's equals, though He Himself created them, and in their ignorance ascribe to Him sons and daughters. Glory to Him! Exalted be he above their imputations! (S. 6:100)

Iblis, angels, and jinn are important in the overall teaching and belief in Islam. Their activities have a serious impact for good or ill upon each individual. From a few extracts from the Koran we have been able to see that it is obvious that their activities are likely to be in the minds of most hospitalized Muslim patients. Awe, fear, penitence, hope, patience, and trust in a merciful and compassionate God are likely to monopolize their thinking. With an awareness of these emotional, mental, and spiritual concerns visitors must sensitively approach Muslim patients.

Chapter 6

Death and the Grave

Hadith means "Tradition" or "Sayings." It refers to the body of recollections of the prophet's sayings and complements the Koran, giving legal advice in matters that the Koran does not touch. They also contain traditions concerning the Prophet's life, which are known as the Sunnah ("way, path, or rule").

It is estimated that as many as 600,000 traditions were amassed. In the mid-ninth century Muhammed al-Bukhari and Muslim ibn al-Hajjaj were deputed to sort through this store and reduce them to two volumes, each of which contain about 4,000 traditions. Later, four less-reliable collections were added.

Until this point the principle of referring only to the Koran had largely been practiced. Often the Hadith, even when commenting on the same subject, are wide and varying. This is no more evident than when the subject of life after death is considered. As in Christianity there are innumerable efforts at personal interpretations of biblical statements concerning postdeath events and eschatology (events of the last days).

First it should be clarified that the death of anyone, irrespective of religious background, depending on the nature of the illness or trauma, is universally similar. From the medical perspective, the death of most people, irrespective of faith and spiritual awareness, is usually peaceful. There are occasions when unrelieved pain causes distress. This distress is not considered due to any religious noncompliance.

It is often the observing, apprehensive, grieving relatives who have the fear of death. They may be in a state of denial, as they do not wish their loved one to die. Death to them is to be delayed as long as possible and is objectionable because of their distaste of the impending judgment. They are the ones who harbor the ideas of and look for signs of death being horrible.

The deep guttural, noisy, gasping sounds heard emanating from some dying patients are spoken of as the "death rattles." They interpret such physical signs as evidence of pain and a fearful death. At this stage the patient is feeling little or no pain and is oblivious of anything else, or they may be in a coma.

The pre-Islamic view of life and death was that a God or several of the many gods created the universe and all that is in it. It was left to run its course without any further interference or interest. In time, there developed the belief that the course of all human life was left in the hands of fate. The early Bedouin belief was that there was a plan for every person's life, which was irrevocably set, as the Koran succinctly expresses:

> They say: "There is this life and no other. We die, and live; nothing but Time destroys us." Surely of this they have no knowledge. They are merely guessing. (S. 45:24)

The same sura offers the Islamic view. God is indeed involved in the functioning of a human life. Not only does God put life into our bodies; he also determines the length of that life. Clearly the teaching is that there is also life beyond death. God is the sovereign ruler of the universe and that includes the earth:

> Say: "It is God who gives you life and later causes you to die. It is He that will gather you on the Day of Resurrection. Of this there is no doubt; yet most men do not know it."
>
> It is God who has sovereignty over the heavens and the earth. On the Day when the hour strikes, those who have denied His revelations will assuredly lose all.
>
> Praise, then, be to God, Lord of the heavens, Lord of the earth, Lord of the Universe. Supremacy be His in the heavens and on the earth. He is the Mighty One, the Wise one. (S. 45:26-28, 37)

The revelations of the Koran turned the pessimistic futility of the harsh nomadic life, which reached its finality in death, to seeing life with a purpose beyond the grave. This new eternal existence will be in the hands of a caring, concerned, and merciful God. The impersonal fate, before the Koran, was overthrown by a divine direction leading to Paradise for those who accept the message it teaches and submit themselves to God. The Koran certainly released a sense of hope yet maintained a fear of what will befall the nonbelievers and hypocrites. Previously there was an unmitigated fear that death was the ultimate destruction. Now in Islam fear, as we have seen, is not bereft of hope. A way of escape is offered for those who sincerely and actively seek to attain an eternity in paradise. For devout Muslims the reality of the future life is always before them. Before this reality, they realize that death and the grave must be experienced.

Before proceeding, it is wise to recognize that there are three types of Muslims among the Muslim community. These types may be observed among those who follow other faiths, whether they are Christians, Hindus, Buddhists, Jews, and so on.

They are:

Nominal Muslims are born into a Muslim family or an Islamic state but do not practice their religion. They have not committed themselves to observing the Five Pillars of Islam. It might be said that they are Muslims by accident. For passport, legal, hospital, or other purposes requiring the declaration of religion, to record "Muslim" is convenient and saves explanations or suspicion. Depending upon their acceptance of the snippets of Islamic knowledge they have picked up, the evidence of fear or indifference to death becomes obvious.

Traditional Muslims usually have some rudimentary knowledge of fundamental Muslim beliefs. When it comes to the practice of the faith they are easily led to less stringent and perhaps more pleasurable ways of living. They still claim allegiance to Islam. Often contact with Western-style living is the temptation. The Territorial Commander in Chief of an army of a Muslim-majority country was my neighbor. In spite of his Islamic profession, the influence of his training at Sandhurst Military College in England was seen. Every week supplies of alcohol, ham, and bacon were flown in for his and his fellow officers' consumption. These are prohibited to a true Muslim. This type of Muslim would be vocal in expressing uncertainty about the future and about a fear of death during the dying process.

True Muslims understand their professed faith and strive to live their lives in accordance with its teaching. By their words and actions they are obedient, loyal, and devoted to their God and the instructions of the Prophet. True Muslims, by the confidence in God—which has been confirmed by accepting his peace and Mercy—enjoy the anticipation that on the Day of Resurrection they will be ushered into Paradise.

So it is with Christians. Nominal Christians are often indifferent when it comes to dying. They don't know and often do not care about death and the grave. Traditional Christians, because of their shallow spiritual knowledge and experience of God, tend to be more apprehensive and fearful about dying. The true Christian waits with joyous anticipation of "being absent from the body and present with the Lord."

Let it be said again. For most people in the period immediately before the final breath there is a calm and peacefulness. The so-called terrors of death are largely the psychological buildup of conditioning by religious and irreligious alike because of a fear of the unknown. Yet when actually encountered, death is experienced as a transition from one state of existence to another. The devout would claim it as the peace of God.

The pastoral caregiver in a health care institution needs to understand the thinking of the average Muslim as to what happens beyond death. The Koran uses the Arabic word "akhira" ("hereafter") 113 times. This word is applied to the existence beyond this earthly life. The intermediate state spent in the grave before the Day of Resurrection is called Barzakh.

Izra'il—the angel of death, separates the soul from the body: "Say: the angel of death in charge of you will reclaim your souls. Then to your Lord will you return." (S. 32:11)

Some of the apprehensions over the dying process arise from the Koran, which describes the angels of death striking the souls of the unbelievers as punishment for their sins.

"If you could see the angels when they carry off the souls of the unbelievers! They shall strike them on their faces and on their backs saying, Taste the torment of the conflagration! This is the punishment for what you have committed! God is not unjust to His servants." (S. 8:50-51)

The burial of the body is usually made within twenty-four hours of the demise. A belief of a continuing relationship between the body and the spirit in the grave is the reason for the objection to autopsies. However, when death becomes a coroner's case the relatives cannot refuse an autopsy. The body is usually interred in a dedicated Muslim cemetery where the deceased's body is able to face Mecca. At the graveside, before the lowering of the body, the ceremony consists of five parts:

1. The proclamation "Allahu Akbar" ("God is Great"), four times with arms raised
2. The reading of Al-Fatihah, Sura 1
3. Recitation of praises to the Prophet
4. Prayers for the Deceased
5. Prayers for the Mourners

The Koran says little concerning the period between death and the Resurrection. The Hadith vary in their presentations of what happens following the separation of body and soul. It is only much later that manuals on eschatology were produced. These provide much of the beliefs concerning the events in the grave.

The spirit leaves the body at death. When the coffin is lowered into the earth God orders the spirit to return to the body for questioning. The work of the interrogators Munkar and Nakir in the postdeath period illustrate more about God's character and his insistence upon justice. Correct responses to their questions are said to open the top of the grave, from which fresh breezes from the Gardens are felt. They are said to be able to overlook those Gardens of Paradise. These manuals emphasize God's mercy and forgiveness.

Al Ghazali tells that on entering the grave the shining-faced Ruman (an angel) asks the deceased to catalog his or her good and bad deeds done during his or her life. The dead protest that there are no writing materials. Ruman orders them to use a finger, their saliva, and their burial clothes and write. The story adds that those burial clothes are hung around the deceased's neck until the Resurrection.[1]

Izutsu relates the story of the Prophet's response to Aisha's (Mohammed wife) distress at hearing of the interrogation in the grave:

> O Aisha, the voice of Munkar and Nakir in the hearing of the believer are like antimony in the eye and the pressure of the tomb to the believer is like the compassionate mother who complains to her of a headache and she strokes his head gently. But, O Aisha, woe to those who doubt God—how they will be squeezed in their graves like the pressure of a boulder on an egg.[2]

The implication of this Hadith is that both the devout and the indifferent will suffer the pressure of the tomb, however only a compassionate God will soothe the believer's pain.

Likewise, the three schools of Islamic thinking—the Traditionalists, the Modernists, and the Spiritualists—also have their differing interpretations of them.

The Traditionalists affirm the writings of earlier scholars as binding for all times, for example, the Talaban and other fundamental extremists. The Modernists present an interpretive analysis of life after death considering contemporary knowledge. The Spiritualists are a reactionary movement arising from British colonialism, Western missionaries, and anthropologists. It is acknowledged that the three sections do not claim exclusiveness.

The Traditionalists see both the body and the soul as being attacked after death. Contemporary Traditionalists accept a freedom of the spirit in the grave yet believe there is still some connection between body and spirit. The dead can feel and do suffer. The dead also are able to hear and respond to the living. For these reasons it is considered a sin to leave the body to medical science. It must also be assumed that the Traditionalist is fearful of the outcome if the whole body cannot be resurrected on the "Day."

The major beliefs of the Traditionalists concerning the state between death and the resurrection are:

1. The agony of death
2. The journey of the spirit to the presence of God
3. The questionings in the grave by Munkar and Nakir
4. Punishment and reward in the tomb
5. The continuing relationship between body and spirit
6. An awareness of the ministrations of the living to the dead

The Traditionalists still adhere to the questionings of Munkar and Nakir. Punishment is an integral part of the Barzakh experience. It is the beginning of the whole process of Judgment. There is debate among contemporary Traditionalists as to whether the spirit assumes the image of the body it inhabited to distinguish it from other spirits.

The Modernists use the methods of research to validate koranic revelations as relevant for modern living. They are more concerned with human responsibility and accountability than the details of life in the grave. Belief in death and resurrection leads to eternal life. Growing, developing, and improving in this life are the ways to establish true Islamic order. Effort is made to help people face death. The death of a loved one brings one to face personal mortality. Death is not the terrifying ordeal of the Traditionalist, rather a stage in the continuum of life. Conditions in the period of Barzakh are beyond comprehension. Dignity and respect for the dead is maintained. Some punishment in Barzakh is possible, as the impurities of sin must be burned out. This fuels their fervent belief that we must start accepting responsibility because, ultimately, accountability has to be faced. Modernist writers are concerned with practical sin. Responsible, ethical living according to the Koran takes away the fear of death.

The Modernists are less concerned in determining the events in the Barzakh period. Their emphasis continues to be in the nature of responsibility and accountability. They preach the message of the meaning of death for the ethical life rather than teaching the details of postdeath conditions, about which none can know.

The suggestion is that the Modernists see the Barzakh not as subject of speculative description but as a direction on how to live one's life now.[3] Thus the fearsomeness is taken out of death. It is presented as a transitional stage in God's revelation of progress toward the Resurrection. Perhaps it may be said that the emphasis is upon death as a rite of passage.

The Modernists note that the Koran says little about the Barzakh happening. They strongly emphasize one of the essential beliefs of Islam that there is a life after death.

The Spiritualists gathered momentum in Egypt through the influence of British spiritualist Sir Oliver Lodge. The dead, who think about us and help us, inhabit the worlds above. They gain support from medieval Islamic writers who wrote on the activities of the spirit in Barzakh. The smile of a newborn babe and the smile of a dying person is considered evidence of a preexistent spiritual life and of being conducted into the spiritual world of the dead by recognized, previously deceased loved ones.

Three types of contactable spirits are recognized: angels, jinn and the spirits of the dead. Jinn are warned against, as in Barzakh they continue their seduction. Basic beliefs of the Spiritualists are:

1. The spirit is alive, comprehending, seeing, and hearing during life in Barzakh.
2. The spirit communicates with other spirits of the dead.
3. The spirit feels bliss or punishment, pleasure or pain according to the deeds it did in the earthly life.
4. Space or any other restrictions do not bind the spirit.
5. The spirit is permitted to communicate with all or part of its former body.
6. The spirits enjoy a high civilization including reading, research, art, entertainment, marriage, and even procreation.

The questionings of Munkar and Nakir are widely accepted amongst Muslims. Ma'sumian[4] and Coward[5] narrate similar accounts of the experience, although there are other versions that may be recounted. These two have been described as black angels with blue eyes (shades of the evil eye idea?). They interrogate the deceased, who are sitting up in the tomb with three critical questions. Who is your God? Who is your Prophet? And what is your faith? If the responses are acceptable the sojourn in the grave will be happy with the grave enlarged seventy times and lighted.

Failure to answer them satisfactorily will result in immediate punishment. Some believe it will to continue to the Day of Judgment. Some report that the grave will shrink in size, putting pressure on the dead body and crushing the ribs. A hideous being without any sensual feeling will begin torture with an iron whip. This will cause some to desire to return to earth, but this will not be possible because of the barrier barring the way. Barzakh means barrier, hence the name of this intermediate state. The deceased are barred from returning to the earth or proceeding to Paradise or Hell.

The Koran provides no evidence for such descriptions except in the matter of alluding to two punishments:

> Some of the desert Arabs around you are hypocrites, and so are some of the citizens of Madinah [Medina], who are indeed fanatical in their hypocrisy. You do not know them, but We know them well. Twice We will chastise them: then they shall return to a grievous torment. (S. 9:101)

> But We would inflict on them the lighter torment of this world before the greater torment of the world to come, so that they may perchance return to the right path. (S. 32:21)

For the average Muslim, death and the grave are important considerations. By such thoughts many are kept close to the chosen path that God had been pleased to reveal to them. It is in the grave that they await the Day of Resurrection.

Chapter 7

Awaiting the Hour of Doom

The status of Barzakh will be interrupted by the "Hour." A strong description of this is given in Sura 22.

> Men have fear of your Lord. The catastrophe of the Hour of Doom shall be terrible indeed.
>
> When that day comes, every suckling mother shall forsake her infant, every pregnant female shall cast her burden, and you shall see men reeling like drunkards although not drunk: such is the horror of God's chastisement.
>
> Yet there are some who in their ignorance dispute about God and follow every rebellious devil, though these are doomed to seduce their followers and lead them to the fire.
>
> Men, if you doubt the Resurrection remember that We first created you from dust, then from a living germ, then from a clot of blood, and then from a half-formed lump of flesh, so that We might manifest to you Our Power.
>
> We cause you to remain in the womb whatever We please for the appointed term, and then We bring you forth as infants, that you may grow up and reach your prime. Some die young and some live on to abject old age when all that they once knew they know no more.
>
> You sometimes see the earth dry and barren: but no sooner do We send the water down upon it than it begins to stir and swell, putting forth every kind of radiant bloom. That is because God is Truth: He resurrects the dead and has power over all things.
>
> The Hour of Doom is sure to come—in this there is no doubt. Those in their graves God will raise to life. (S. 22:1-7)

Before the actual "Day" there will occur a series of events. These events will culminate in what, as we have seen, the Koran calls "The Hour of Doom." God alone knows the time. It will be sudden. As the Christians believe, "in the twinkling of an eye."

> People ask you about the Hour of Doom. Say: "God alone has knowledge of it. Who knows? It may well be that the hour is at hand." (S. 33:63)

> Lost indeed are those who deny they will ever meet God. When the Hour of Doom overtakes them unawares, they will exclaim: "Alas, we have neglected much in our lifetime!" And they shall bear the burdens on their backs. Evil are the burdens they shall bear. (S. 6:29-31)

These passages echo the words of Jesus, in Matthew Chapter 26 and Luke Chapter 12, and the Christian perception of the end times. They also echo Zoroastrian beliefs. The so-called "Second Coming of Christ" obsesses some sections of the Christian church. Other practical aspects of Christian teaching and practice are neglected as they seek to interpret signs and make their own prophecies concerning the event and the timing of the Hour. Similarly, Muslims are attracted to the speculative elements concerning the Hour. The traditions are loaded with speculations about the state of the world prior to and the events that give rise to God's intervention on that day.

The Koran does give some vague clues to keep the believer alert to the need to remain in a constant relationship of 'submission' to God and right living pleasing to him. Jewish, Christian, and Muslim scriptures all indicate that the Hour is near at hand.

The Sovereign God is leading all human history to the eschaton (the last days). He has given a forewarning of cosmic and moral signs that will herald the Hour of Doom. Sections of Christians, for two millennia, have periodically set dates for the Day of Resurrection. Many have sold earthly possessions and disposed of them and waited. Each time the day passed without excitement and they continued to live with embarrassed faces and a teetering faith. Similarly, Zoroastrians have had detailed itineraries of events which brought frustration, despair, and a rescheduling of another time-table.

The Koran and the Hadith speak of cataclysmic events that will take place when natural laws of the Universe will be thrown into chaos.

> When the sky is rent apart, obeying her Lord in true submis-sion; when the earth expands and casts out all that is within her and becomes empty, obeying her Lord in true submission; then, O man, who labor constantly to meet your Lord, shall you meet Him.
>
> He that is given his book in his right hand shall be given le-nient reckoning, and shall go back rejoicing to his people. But he that is given his book behind his back shall call down destruction upon himself and burn in the fire of Hell; for he lived without care amongst his people and thought he would never return to God. Yes; but his Lord was ever watching him. (S. 82:1-14)

> But when the sight of mortals is confounded and the moon eclipsed; when sun and moon are brought together—on that day men will ask: "Whither shall I flee?"
>
> No, there shall be no refuge. For to your Lord, on that day, shall you return. (S. 75:5-11)

> The Supreme Terror shall not grieve them, and the angels will receive them, saying: "this is the day you have been promised."
>
> On that day We shall rollup the heaven like a scroll of parchment. Just as We brought the first creation into being, so will We restore it. This is a promise We shall assuredly fulfill. (S. 21:103-105)

> The Hour of Doom is drawing near, and the moon is cleft in two. Yet, when they see a sign, the unbelievers turn their backs and say: "Ingenious sorcery." (S. 54:1)

But what are the signs of the approaching Hour? These words spoken by Gabriel to the Prophet suggest that the earth, the heaven, and all that is therein shall be devastatingly destroyed. All the natural laws that God invoked shall be reversed. This disruption of God's natural order affects all. The sun's illuminatory gift to the earth will be removed. Stars will fall from their orbits. Earthquakes and volcanoes shall flatten mountains. The oceans will boil from the heat of those volcanic rampages. Domestic animal life shall be forsaken because people will be so terrified that material property and wealth will have no significance. The panic among "man-eating" beasts will sedate their savagery till they are become like domesticated pets. These natural calamities, suggest Smith and Haddad, are paralleled in the Hadith.[1] These authors describe the moral degeneracy that will flourish even in Muslim communities prior to the Hour. This disintegration of the integrity of society is similar to the Christian description of the reign of the anti-Christ, when the mark of the beast shall be emblazoned on the forehead of the disobedient before Christ overthrows and defeats the beast. The "rolling up of the heavens like a scroll of parchment" in Sura 21 is interpreted to mean that the seven hells and the seven stages of Paradise will be revealed for the first time to ordinary humans (prophets and martyrs excepted).

In the Koran, Gog and Magog of the Christian book of Revelation are creaturely associates of evil in this period. They will remain damned up until the dam is burst at the end of time. Then, they will come flooding down to lead humans astray.

> Then he followed yet another route until he came between Two Mountains and found people who could barely understand a word. "Dhul-Qarnayn," they said, "Gog and Magog are ravaging this land. Build us a rampart between us, and we will pay you tribute."
>
> He replied, "The power my Lord has given me is greater than tribute. Lend me a force of men, and I will raise a rampart between you and them. Come bring me blocks of iron."
>
> He damned up the valley between the Two Mountains and said, "Ply your bellows." And when their iron blocks were red with heat he said, "Bring me molten brass to pour on them."
>
> Gog and Magog could not scale it, nor could they dig their way through it. He said: "This is a blessing from my Lord.

But when my Lord's promise has been fulfilled, He will level it to dust. The promise of my Lord is true." (S. 18:92-98)

It is ordained that no nation We have destroyed shall ever rise again. But when Gog and Magog are let loose and rush down every hill; when the true promise nears its fulfilment; unbelievers will stare in amazement, crying: "Woe to us! Of this we have been heedless. We have assuredly done wrong." (S. 21:95-97)

Gog and Magog are destructive creatures who will oppose God and his anointed One. The Jewish prophet Ezekiel's visions of the last days sees them involved when the forces of evil are overthrown and God's kingdom is established. They appear in post-exilic Jewish literature as rebels against God. Like a scourge they will sweep down from the broken dam upon the earth. They will conquer the minds of humans and hurl abuse at God. Gog and Magog are associated alongside Dajjal, who is the anti-Christ. Dajjal will lead humankind into moral anarchy. He will usher in the period of the great tribulation, enticing multitudes to follow him.

Shi'a tradition says that he will come from a far island. He will be one-eyed with letters KFR (kafir, meaning infidel) stamped on his face. His rule will last for forty years (others suggest forty days). Protective walls of angels will stop his victory march into Mecca and Medina.[2]

The Koran refers to the rising of the "beast of the earth" at this time. "On the day when the Doom overtakes them We will bring out from the earth a monster that shall speak to them. Truly, men have no faith in our revelations" (S. 27:83).

There is no consistent understanding of the role of the beast. It is not usually identified with being Dajjal, but is interpreted as being some kind of huge creature that will bear witness to the unfaithful about the Power of God. He is believed by some to brand the faces of men to identify nonbelievers from believers.[3] Here we see agreement and disagreement with the Shi'a position. They agree in relation to Dajjal but differ in their references to the beast of the earth.

There seems to be little support for identifying Dajjal with Iblis the fallen angel (Satan). Some claim, however, that Dajjal *is* Satan or one of his manifestations. Dajjal's success in seducing many, including Muslims, is because of his resemblance to the Christ. This seduction is successful because they are convinced that he is the expected returning Messiah. One of the clear signs of the approaching hour is that during the reign of Dajjal, Jesus (Isa) will return to battle with and defeat Dajjal.

> He is a portent of the Hour of Doom. Have no doubt about its coming and follow me. This is the straight path: let not Satan mislead you, for he is your inveterate foe.
>
> And when Jesus came with evident signs, he said, "I have come to give you wisdom, and to make plain to you some of the things you differ about. Fear God and follow me. God is my Lord and your Lord: therefore serve Him. That is the straight path."
>
> Yet the factions disagreed among themselves. But woe to the wrongdoers when they suffer the anguish on the woeful day.
>
> Are they waiting for the Hour of Doom to overtake them unawares, without warning? Friends on that day shall become enemies to one another. Except the God-fearing. (S. 43:57-69)

There is some linguistic debate on the Arabic meaning of this passage. Many scholars accept that it is a reference that Isa's coming is a sign of the Hour.

Al Ghazali says that former prophets inhabit the seven heavens. Jesus' station is in the fifth heaven. Ghazali proposes that five have liberty to move where they like in the heavens: Abraham, Moses, Jesus, Adam, and Mohammed. The rest are to remain in their places until the "Hour."

It will be in the fortieth year or day, (according to the tradition followed), that Jesus will return to annihilate Dajjal, establishing his own Kingdom for forty years. Ma'sumian describes this rule as one of "happiness, love and prosperity for all humanity."[4]

One of the larger factions of Islam is the twelve shi'as who propound that prior to the general resurrection of the Hour another holy personage will appear, Al-Mahdi. He will end the period of tribulation created by Dajjal, bringing peace and justice. One tradition traces his genealogy back to the Prophet himself. His earthly rule will be for seven years. Some of the traditions equate Isa with Mahdi. Others see them as cooperatively overthrowing Dajjal. There are those who seem to ignore the role of Isa, leaving all the rescue of mankind from this great deception to Mahdi.

The Hadith vary as to the location where the arrival of Jesus' second coming will occur. Some predict it to be at the Great Mosque of Damascus, Jerusalem, or other parts of the Arab world. Generally, the coming of Isa and the Mahdi are separate events.

Smith and Haddad cite Ibn Khaldum who is uncertain as to whether Isa or Isa and Mahdi together will kill Dajjal.[5] The confusion over these two and their part in the eschaton has been made more complex by political situations intruding into the interpretations. The prediction of the Mahdi's rule on earth varies between five, seven, and nine years. Similarly, the descriptions of the Mahdi are confusing. The role of the Mahdi is that of reformer rather than prophet. Most of the Hadith concerning the Mahdi claim the authority of the Prophet himself. It is doubtful whether he actually visualized such a figure. The numbers of references to the Madhi in the Hadith has firmly established him as one of the significant signs of the Hour, along with the sun rising in the west.

The apostle Paul's early position on the second coming of Jesus in II Thessalonians speaks of the trumpet blast declaring the Day of Resurrection. Trumpets also will feature in the heralding in of the "Hour of Doom" in Islam. In this belief, the Koran provides much support. The Hadith again contributes by introducing the archangel Israfil as the trumpeter. The Koran, with two exceptions, speaks of one trumpet blast only.

> It is he who created the heavens and the earth in all truth. On the day when He says: "Be" it shall be. His word is truth. All sovereignty shall be His on the Day when the trumpet is sounded. He has knowledge of the unknown and the manifest. He alone is Wise and All-knowing. (S. 6:73)

> On that Day We shall let them come in tumultuous throngs. The trumpet shall be sounded and We shall gather them all. (S. 18:100)

> When the trumpet is sounded, on that day their ties of kindred shall be broken, nor shall they ask help of one another. (S. 23:101)

> The trumpet will be blown and, behold, they will rise up from their graves and hasten to their Lord. "Woe to us!" they will say. "Who has roused us from our resting place? This is what the Lord of Mercy has promised: the apostles have told the truth!" And with but one blast they shall be gathered all before Us. (S. 36:50-52)

> Yet these are waiting for but one single blast—the blast which no one can retard. They say, "Lord, hasten our doom before the Day of Reckoning comes!" (S. 38:18)

> Fixed is the Day of Judgment. On that day the trumpet shall be sounded, and you shall come in multitudes. The gates of Heaven shall swing open, and the mountains shall pass away and become like vapor." (S. 78:17-19)

> But when the dread blast is sounded, on that day each man will forsake his brother, his mother and father, his wife and his children: for each of them on that day will have enough sorrow of his own. (S. 80:39-40)

In these verses the message is clear that the trumpet will sound. The cataclysmic disintegration of the earth will be completed and all will be gathered (those in Barzakh and those still living) before the Lord. The whole is a frightening picture, particularly for the unfaithful who will realize their foolishness in not heeding the word of the Prophet.

The Koran also speaks of two blasts:

> The trumpet shall be sounded, and all who are in the heavens and on earth shall fall down fainting, except those that are spared by God. The trumpet will be blown again and they shall rise and gaze around them. The earth will shine in the light of her Lord, and the book will be laid open. The prophets and the witnesses shall be brought in, and all will be

judged with fairness: none shall be wronged. Every soul shall be paid back according to his deeds, for He knows best all that they did. (S. 39:67-70)

By those who snatch away men's souls, and those who gently release them, and those who speed headlong; by those who govern the affairs of this world! On the day the trumpet sounds its first and second blast, and all eyes shall stare with awe.
They say: "When we have turned to hollow bones, shall we be restored to life? A fruitless transformation!" But with one blast they shall return to the earth's surface. (S. 79:1-14)

In the fourteenth verse of Sura 79 "returning to the earth's surface" may be understood as "being awakened." It requires only one blast of the trumpet to resurrect them.

There are some traditions that speak of Israfil blowing the trumpet three times. Ma'sumian refers to Hughes' *Dictionary of Islam,* which suggests that the first blast is that of "consternation."[6] By this the heaven's and the earth's creatures will be terror-stricken as the cosmic world is shattered.

The second blast is that of "examination." The third and final trumpet sound will call forth the resurrection of all the human dead.

For our purpose—that of gaining some understanding of the average Muslim's mind concerning the last days and the "Hour of Doom"—it is wise to restrict ourselves to the basic position of the Koran. The heralding of the trumpet will proclaim the final stages of the hour by the Archangel Israfil. There may be one of two trumpet blasts. By the trumpeting, the catastrophic reversal of the laws of nature will be simultaneous with the resurrection of the dead, who will gather with those who remained alive at the call of the "Hour."

Chapter 8

The Day of Resurrection

A life of submission to the Holy, Almighty, Merciful, and Compassionate God will reach its culmination point on the Day of Resurrection. It is a day to be feared, a day to be anticipated, a day to be filling the faithful with hope. Christians believe in the Day of Resurrection, but really pay scant attention to it by comparison with their Muslim brothers and sisters. As in Christianity, the Day of Judgment is for the Muslims also a Day of Accountability. Sadly, many Christians have neglected to keep in mind the awesomeness of this coming day. Their emphasis on the loving nature of God has lulled many of them into an apathy and complacency concerning it. All peoples, of whatever religious allegiance, will have to face "the Day." In religions that accept the Karma principle of Cause and Effect (i.e., "What you sow you reap in the next life") there also is a belief in accountability when they die. In their belief they are reincarnated into a higher or lower life form according to the way they conducted themselves in the life just completed. An almost universal belief exists that beyond this life a time of reckoning must be faced. Even the harshest critic would not be able to dispute that one of the basic messages of the Koran and Islam is that persons will be called to account for their actions and evidence of their faith, which they presented throughout their lives. Because of this, the Islamic message is that all must submit themselves to God in order to safeguard themselves against a negative judgment on the Day.

The day is known as the "Day of Resurrection" or the "Day of Reckoning." These two titles sum up the basic functions of the Day. First, the bodies of the dead will be resurrected and reunified with their spirits. The second is that these revived, whole, responsible beings will face their final judgment. It will be recalled that the angels Munkar and Nakir questioned them in the grave concerning their faith and certain punishments were meted out there. This second judgment will assess the quality of their lives and faith and assign them to their places in their eternal abode. This is consistent with the teaching in the Koran and Islam, which stresses human responsibility and human accountability. In this section we will look at the accounting, the crossing of the bridge, and the situation beyond the judgment.

We have already read about how the trumpets will blast, triggering the disintegration of the cosmic world and summoning the dead and the living before God. The Koran suggests that all will perish in that moment—only God will stand, alone:

> Invoke no other god but God. There is no god but Him. All things shall perish except Him. He is the Judgment and to Him you shall be called. (S. 28:88)

> All that lives on the face of the earth is doomed to die. But the face of your Lord will abide for ever, in all its majesty and glory. Which of your Lord's blessings would you deny? (S. 55:26-27)

Classical Islam appears to infer that there will be an indefinite period in which the starkness of the emptiness sinks in before God actually reunites bodies and spirits. Then they will be brought face to face with Him. Smith and Haddad acknowledge the uncertainty of this period and refer to the description of Al Ghazali, who then sees God opening one of His treasure houses from which pour the sea of life onto the barren ground generating new life.[1] When the earth is covered with two meters of water the regrowth of individual bodies will begin in the graves, until the form of the deceased person will be assumed as at the time of death.

Neither the Koran nor the Hadith provide us with a reliable chronology of these events. There is no doubt about the fact that there will be a resurrection.

> "What!" they say, "When we are turned to bone and dust shall we be restored to a new creation?"

Say: "Whether you turn to stone or iron, or any other substance you may think unlikely to be given life."

They will ask, "Who will restore us?"

Say: "He that created you first."

They will shake their heads and ask: "When will this be?"

Say: "It may be near at hand. On that day He will summon you all, and you shall answer Him with praises. You shall think that you have stayed away for a little while." (S. 17:50-52)

"What!" says man, "When I am once dead, shall I be raised to life?"

Does man forget that We created him when he was nothing before? By the Lord, We will call to account in company with all the devils and set them on their knees around the fire of Hell: from every sect We will carry off the stoutest rebels against the Lord of Mercy. We surely know best who deserves most to be burnt therein. (S. 19:68-70)

I swear by the Day of Resurrection, and by the self reproaching soul!

Does man think We shall never put his bones together again? Indeed, we can remold his very fingers!

Yet man would ever deny what is to come. "When will this be," he asks, "this Day of Resurrection?" (S. 75:1-5)

Consensus suggests that Israfil will be the first to be restored to life, after which he will blow the trumpet to call the dead back to life. The passages of the Koran cited show that God animates the dead and summons them into His presence for the Judgment. After Israfil, Abraham, Moses, or Mohammed is the next to be resurrected, although they are also said to have stations in Heaven before the Day. Mohammed's early resurrection before the other prophets is considered evidence of his status before God and the importance of his role as intercessor before God on behalf of Muslims.

Some traditions give accounts of animals being raised, including the horse ridden by Mohammed the night he visited Jerusalem and the heavens. Others speak of the equality of the resurrected before God, as they will be all naked, barefooted, and uncircumcised, suggesting powerlessness. Their differentiation is seen in the lights they carry. The brightness of their lamps is proportional to their faith and the quality of their deeds. The rate of their progress to God is similarly determined. The faster they move the more acceptable their lives. People will ride, walk, or crawl according to their works. One Hadith claims that the Assembly will be at Jerusalem while another puts it halfway between earth and heaven.

WEIGHED IN THE BALANCES

Earlier Sura 9:19-31 was quoted, in which the favorably judged would be given the "this is your life" book in their right hands while the others would receive it behind their backs. The following verses confirm this idea.

> The fate of each man We have bound about his neck. On the Day of Resurrection We will confront him with the book spread wide open, saying: "Here is your book: read it. Enough for you this day that your own soul shall call you to account.".... (S. 17:13)

> The Day will surely come when We shall summon every nation with its apostle. Those who are given their books in their right hands will read their recorded doings, and shall not in the least be wronged. But those who have been blind in this life, shall be blind in the life to come and go further astray. (S. 17:71-73)

Traditions vary widely concerning the details of the events regarding the handing over of the books and their judgment. A commonly held classical view, based on the above verse from Sura 17, is that the record is hung about the neck in the grave. Others imply that at the resurrection it is handed either to the right or the left hand according to the life of faith lived.

There are traditions that relate how each is brought before the Mizan (balance or scales), upon which the books are weighed. It is assumed that the accounts of the good deeds are in the right-side pan and the bad deeds in the left. Such a portrayal emphasizes the equity of God's judgments. Any protest by a person judged negatively as being unfair, will be futile.[2]

> "Peace!" shall be the word spoken by a Merciful God. But to the guilty He will say: "Away with you this day! Sons of Adam, did I not charge you never to worship Satan, your acknowledged foe, but to worship Me? Surely that is the straight path. Yet he has led a multitude of you astray. Had you no sense? This is the Hell you have been threatened with. Burn therein this day on account of your unbelief."
> "On that day We shall seal their mouths . . . " (S. 36:58-65)

The classical interpretations seem to favor the concept that the original body of bones and flesh will be reconstituted as it stands before the Mizan with the books. A large sector of the Modernists discounts this view. The new body will be similar in appearance but different in composition. The joys and blessings of the Garden could not be fully appreciated and indulged in with purely human components. The delights of the Gardens are beyond human comprehension; therefore a "body of clay" is inadequate. Another argument is that if heaven and earth are completely changed by the "Day," then it is difficult to understand how the human's body will remain the same. Many Muslims still accept the resurrection of the natural body, basing it on the reference in Sura 69:24, in which those judged righteous are invited to eat and drink at their leisure. Others argue that a physically resurrected body is needed to experience the horrors of the fires of Hell. A variant to this is the concept that the bodies of the righteous are spiritual and eternal while those of the unfaithful are physical and temporary.

The Spiritualists' view is that the rewards and punishments will be apportioned immediately after death and that the bodies in the Barzakh are the spiritual forms that will experience the Gardens or Hell.

Another group of interpreters claim that Heaven and Hell are states, not localities. Latif sees Hell as being "a state of the soul whose faculties are defective, diseased and whose reactions are painful in contrast with the pleasant agreeable reactions of the healthy soul."[3] He points out that our consideration of these matters employs physical images because that is the only type of life we have experienced.

Many take a position maintaining a middle ground between the extremes of the physical and spiritual perception of the resurrected body. Whatever the view of the composition condition of the resurrected taken by Modern Muslims, they all see it as providing an incentive. This is the encouragement to be constantly aware that we are accountable, all of our earthly days, for the way we live and practice our faith in preparation for the Day.

THE BRIDGE

In Zoroastrianism the "Bridge of Chinvat" is similar to a flat sword blade upon which the individual walks. As he walks, the list of his or her good and bad deeds are read out. If the deeds warrant Hell then the blade slowly tips up, narrowing the walking space until only the razor sharp edge of the blade is there. The plunge is into the abyss of Hell or, as it is called, the "House of Lies" forever. Zoroaster himself will guide the righteous across the bridge into Paradise—"The House of Song."

The name of the Bridge in Islam is Sirat or the "Bridge of Reckoning." Ma'sumian, quoting a Hadith, describes the bridge as "thinner than a hair and sharper than a sword."[4] The most righteous will walk across with poise, while the less righteous will need to crawl across. The sinful will labor under a load of guilt and fall into the pit. Some believers will be too frightened to approach the bridge. Angels will intervene and help these souls cross the bridge through leaping flames. The similarities with the Chinvat Bridge are obvious.

References to Sirat in the Koran are indefinite. Only two verses referring to the "Path" (Sirat) have been seen to refer to the "Bridge."

> On that day We shall seal their mouths. Their hands will speak to Us, and their feet will testify to their misdeeds. Had it been Our will, We could have put out their sight: yet even then they would have rushed headlong upon their wonted *path*. For how could they have seen their error? (S. 36:67-68; emphasis added)

But We shall say: "Call the sinners and their spouses, and the idols which they worshipped besides God, and lead them to the *path* of Hell. Keep them there for questioning. But what has come over you that you cannot help one another." (S. 37:24-25; emphasis added)

Both the blessed and the condemned are to cross the bridge. Hadith again vary as to the sequence of events. Some suggest that the angel Jibril (Gabriel) will guard the approach to the bridge and Mikhail (Michael) will be stationed in the middle to question them. The more popular classical view is that God makes a speedy crossing possible for those who have already been destined for Paradise. The sinful will fall into the fires of Hell. For a purification period the faithless or outright sinful are flung into the eternal flames. Another Hadith describes the bridge as having seven arches, each spanning 3,000 years. On each, according to Smith and Haddad, they will be questioned about their faith (Iman), their prayer life (Salat), their almsgiving (Zakat), their ritual ablutions (Ghusl), and their responsibility toward relatives and community.[5]

The Spiritualists see no need for the Bridge as for them the issuing of punishments and rewards take place immediately after death. They view death as a second birth.

THE LIFE BEYOND

The Koran is unequivocal—there are but two destinations decreed because of the Judgment. There are no alternatives. The unfaithful plummet from the bridge. The faithful are led into the Gardens of Paradise. The Koran speaks much of both. The Hadith go into some extravagant descriptions, particularly of the state of those in Paradise. Hell is described as being brought out of the dust. After the earth has been ground to dust on the "Day," it will become a place of punishment.

No! But when the earth is crushed to fine dust, and your Lord comes down with the angels, in their ranks, and Hell is brought near—on that day man will remember his deeds. But what will memory avail him? (S. 89:21-24)

Hell is a place where the fires burn eternally and are being refueled constantly with boiling water that is available around it.

> Those whom God guides are rightly guided; but those whom He confounds shall find no friends besides Him. We shall gather them all on the Day of Resurrection, prostrate upon their faces, blind, dumb, and deaf. Hell shall be their home: whenever its flames die down We shall rekindle them into a greater fire. (S. 17:97)

> This is the Hell which sinners deny. They shall wander between fire and water fiercely seething. Which of the Lord's blessings would you deny? (S. 55:44)

> Say: "Those of old and those of the present age shall be brought together on the appointed day. As for sinners who deny the truth, you shall eat the fruit of the Zaqqum tree and fill your bellies with it. You shall drink scalding water: yet you shall drink it as the thirsty camel drinks." (S. 56:50-54)

> When they are flung into the flames, they shall hear it roaring and seething, as though bursting with rage. And every time a multitude is thrown therein, its keepers will say to them: "Did no one come to warn you?" "Yes," they will reply, "he did come, but we rejected him and said, God has revealed nothing: you are in grave error." And they will say, "If only we had listened and understood, we should not now be among the heirs of the fire."
> Thus shall they confess their sin. Far from God's mercy are the heirs of the Fire. (S. 67:7-11)

There are seven names given to this place of torment, which the Koran does not name. It does state that it has seven gates.

> He replied, "This is My straight path. You shall have no power over My servants, only the sinners who follow you. They are all destined for Hell. It has seven gates, and through each gate they shall come in separate bands." (S.15:43-45)

From this developed the concept of seven levels of Hell, each level descending to a more dreadful and fearsome torment. The Hadith evolved elaborate systems of punishments such as: purgatorial fire for Muslims; flaming fire for Christians; raging fire for the Jews; blazing fire for the Sabaens; scorching fire for Magi; and the abyss for the hypocrites.[6] Angels, not devils, guard each gate while others supervise the torture of the damned. After a time within the purgatorial fires pardon will be granted and they will be translated to Paradise. Then the purgatorial fire will be extinguished. Some traditions add that Mohammed will weep for these Muslims who shall have to endure this temporary fire.

Death in Hell is impossible. Inhabitants' clothes will be covered in pitch, as will be their faces, to ensure that the pain is more excruciating.

> And when they called for help, every hardened sinner came to grief.
>
> Hell will stretch before him, and putrid water shall he drink; he will sip but scarcely swallow. Death will assail him from every side, yet he shall not die. Harrowing torment awaits him.
>
> On the day when the earth is changed into a different earth and the heavens into new heavens, mankind shall stand before God, the One, who conquers all. On that day you shall see the guilty bound in chains, their garments blackened with pitch and their face covered with flames.
>
> God will reward each soul according to his deeds. Swift is God's reckoning. (S. 14:15-17, 50)

Escape is impossible, as they will be in chains thirty-five meters long.

> We shall say: "Lay hold of him and bind him. Burn him in the fire of Hell, then fasten him with chain seventy cubits long. For he did not believe in God, the Most Great, nor did he care to feed the destitute. Today he shall be friendless here; filth shall be his food, the filth which sinners eat." (S. 69:30-35)

More terrors are given in Sura 22:19-21:

> Garments of fire have been prepared for the unbelievers. Scalding water shall be poured on their heads, melting their skins and that which is in their bellies. They shall be lashed with rods of iron.
>
> Whenever, in their anguish, they try to escape from Hell, back they shall be dragged, and will be told: "Taste the torment of conflagration."

The Hadith produce even more gruesome accounts of the state of those in Hell.

The Modernists, such as Muhammad Zafrullah Khan do not see Heaven and Hell as separate regions, but Hell to be the state of the soul that is functionally deformed, experiencing hurtful and deplorable feelings. This is in line with many Modernists who see the resurrection not to be that of a physical body of flesh and bones but a spiritual body. Muhammad Iqbal writes, "The descriptions in the Koran are visible representations of an inner fact, i.e., character. Hell in the words of the Koran is 'God's kindled fire, which mounts above the hearts'—the painful realization of one's failure as a man."[7]

Many modern scholars try to maintain a position between the extremely gruesome physical punishments and the purely spiritual understanding of the Hell condition. Some suggest that the suffering is psychological. Others see the pains of Hell to be both spiritual and sensual. Some of those of the Modern school suggest that the scriptural interpretation demands a symbolic approach.

Reality for the condemned following Judgment, as seen by both the Traditionalists and the Modernists, will be that of suffering and regret for the failure to heed the warnings of the prophets to live a life of submission to God.

The other side of the coin is the Paradise scene. As we have seen, Paradise is the reward for those who have sincerely lived according to God's laws and have shown true repentance. They have received God's pardon. The koranic description of Hell has been portrayed to deter disobedience to God's word. The colorful scene it paints of Paradise is meant to draw us to consider the delightful consequences of obedience to God's word. The vivid description of Paradise expressed in the beautiful poetic hymn Sura 55 is seen in the reply to the question, "which are the favors of the Lord would you deny *[yourself]*?" The following quotation of Sura 55:45-76 omits the question above asked at the end of each verse.

> But for those that fear the Majesty of their Lord there are two gardens . . . planted with shady trees. . . .
> Each is watered by a flowing spring. . . .
> Each bears every kind of fruit in pairs. . . .
>   They recline on couches lined with thick brocade and within reach will hang the fruit of both gardens. . . .
> Therein are bashful virgins whom neither man nor jinnee will have touched before. . . .
> Virgins as fair as coral rubies. . . .
> Shall the reward of goodness be anything but good?. . .
> And beside these there shall be two gardens . . . of darkest green. . .
> A gushing fountain shall flow in each. . . .
> Each planted with fruit trees, the palm and the pomegranate. . . .
> In each there will be virgins chaste and fair. . . .
> Dark-eyed virgins sheltered in their tents . . . whom neither man nor jinnee will have touched before. . . .
> They shall recline on green cushions and fine carpets.

Those who will reside in those gardens are also revealed in the Koran.

> As for those that have faith and do good works, they shall forever dwell on the gardens of Paradise, desiring no change to befall them. (S. 18:107-108)

> Blessed are the believers, who are humble in their prayers; who avoid profane talk and give alms to the destitute; who restrain their carnal desires (except with their wives and slave girls for these are lawful to them . . . who are true to their trusts and promises, and are diligent in their prayers. These are the heirs of Paradise. . . . (S. 23:1-5)

Reminiscent of the description of Hell, Paradise is to have seven paths or strata.

> You shall surely die hereafter, and be restored to life on the Day of Resurrection. We have created seven heavens above you; of Our creation. We are never heedless. (S. 23:16-17)

This concept, again, is found in early Babylonian beliefs. The Christian Paul speaks in 1 Corinthians, Chapter 12 of being physically or by vision caught up to the highest heaven. In Christian circles there is talk without details of seven heavens. In the Koran it is described as beautiful for those whose lives are wholesome and patient:

> These shall be rewarded for their fortitude with the highest abode in Paradise. There they shall find a greeting and a welcome, and there they shall abide for ever: a blessed dwelling and a blessed resting place. (S. 25:76-77)

The Hadith describe the highest garden as being under God's throne and from it flow the four rivers of Paradise. Others name the uppermost part of Heaven as the Garden of Eden. Reference has been made to Sura 55, in which two gardens are mentioned. In the description that follows, the items selected are described as being in pairs. This sura has fueled speculation that there are four gardens. During the Middle Ages the concept of seven Gardens was firmly established. These were: the Abode of the Garden (pearl); the Abode of Peace (red sapphire); the Garden of Refuge (green chrysolite); the Garden of Eternity (yellow coral); the Garden of Bliss (silver); the Garden of Firdaws (red gold); and the Garden of Eden (white pearl). The use of precious stones is found also in the Christian Book of Revelation to describe Heaven.

During the Upper Room discourse, Jesus stated that in Heaven there would be many mansions. At least one tradition of Islam states that there are 1,000 rooms in each. Many Hadith describe the sensual pleasures to be enjoyed in the Garden. Hur (chaste women) are promised to men in Sura 55. These Hur or Houri (singular) are different from female believers in the Gardens. Many Hadith describe men being waited upon by Hur, women and virgins numbering in various counts up to many thousands each. These descriptions have been used to condemn Islam as being sensually orientated and sexist. Such criticism misses the point of the expounders of such conditions for believers in the Garden. Such extreme pictures of delights, joys, peace, pleasure, and tranquility in Paradise are to spur all on, with greater enthusiasm in their striving for a safe passage across the bridge into the Garden.

WOMEN AND CHILDREN IN THE AFTERLIFE

The West has denigrated Islam for many of its misconceptions concerning the abuse of women. Let it be honestly stated that the Koran says more about the equality of women on earth and their accountability to God than does the New Testament. Only in the later half of the twentieth century are Christian women being given greater recognition and authority in the Church. This affirms that Christianity has been unashamedly chauvinistic, even in the way the Christian scriptures have been translated from the original Greek and Hebrew.

No society is perfect in its behavior. In Western Christian-majority countries more moral decadence and rape occurs than in Islamic societies. This is even allowing for the fact that the "Shame" factor in the Arab Culture is apt to cover up many such wrongs or even prevent them. Islam endeavors to keep a tight rein on moral behavior within those communities. The penalties for such breeches are severe.

Many of us can cite personal knowledge of atrocities performed by nominal Christian and nominal Muslims. Having lived in countries and areas in which one or another group is in the majority I know this to be true. Before being judgmental of a religion because of what some of its adherents do, we must keep in mind the revealed teachings expounded by that religion's founder and other authentic prophets. The whole must not be condemned because of the behavior of a few.

This equality of men and women will never be more transparent than on the Day of Reckoning:

> But the believers who do good works, both men and women, shall enter Paradise. They shall not suffer the least injustice. (S. 4:124)

> God will surely punish the hypocrites and the idolaters, both men and women; but to believing men and believing women He shall show mercy. God is forgiving and merciful. (S. 33:73)

The faithless wives of Lot and Noah will be consigned to the fire. The wife of Pharaoh, who saved Moses from the massacre of Hebrew babies may expect a place in the Garden.

> God has set an example to the unbelievers in the wife of Noah and the wife of Lot. They were married to two of our righteous servants and deceived them. Their husbands could in no way protect them from God. They were told: Enter the fire with those that shall enter it.
> But to the faithful, God has set an example in Pharaoh's wife, who said: "Lord, build me a house with You in Paradise and deliver me from the wicked Pharaoh and his misdeeds. Deliver me from a wicked nation." (S. 66:10-11)

Modern writers and commentators concur that wives are not considered as being punishable for their husbands' lack of faith. Hadith again vary on this subject, some going so far as to suggest that the majority of women will be in the fire.

Concerning children in the afterlife the Koran has again little to say. Two verses are cited referring to children in Paradise. In Sura 13 the reference is to those who are obedient to God:

> These shall have the reward of Paradise, They shall enter the gardens of Eden, together with the righteous among their fathers, their wives, and their descendants. From every gate the angels will come to them, saying: "Peace be to you for all you

have steadfastly endured. Blessed is the reward of Paradise."
(S. 13:23-24)

(We shall unite true believers with those of their descendants who follow them in the faith, and shall not deny them the reward of their good works; each man is the hostage of his own deeds.) (S. 52:21)

Contemporary commentators on these verses stress that the presence of relatives in Paradise is on the same level with the deceased—because they are virtuous and it makes the departed happy. Children are in the Garden because of mutual faith. It is said that children who die before the age of discretion will avoid the Barzakh and directly enter Paradise. This claim also applies to an aborted fetus, which will have the appearance of a person forty years of age.

A tradition of Al Ghazali suggests that a parent gains automatic entry into the Garden if three children have predeceased the parent. This is based on tradition, not the Koran, that deceased children in the garden are able to intercede on behalf of the parent before Mohammed. One of the negative outcomes of such a belief is the willingness to send offspring into battle in a Holy War.

POSTDEATH EXPERIENCE

How should a pastoral caregiver expect a Muslim patient to react to postdeath experience?

A common Sufi practice was to build villages in view of the cemetery to remind them of the resurrection. Hazrat Inayat Khan sees in such an action that the Sufis, through their mysticism, sought to master "out of body" experiences to prove their mastery over death before physical death takes place.[8] This is not the position of the average modern Muslim. The Koran and secular traditions continue to influence their thinking. There remains the argument regarding dichotomy of body and spirit or the unity of body and spirit in eschaton, both having their strong protagonists. Does the deceased have a spiritual body in the resurrection or the same body of flesh and blood? That is their question.

On this question of the resurrection of the body, modern Muslims take the middle approach. A full bodily or a purely spiritual resurrection are both acceptable beliefs. Notwithstanding the natural decomposition of the human body, God, if he chose, could reassemble scattered parts in conformity with rational and natural laws. Thus a physical and a spiritual resurrection body is acceptable, the details of which are beyond human comprehension. It is not the place of the caregiver to dispute the merits of either position. Christians have faced the same inability to know. Until recent years some Christians groups would not permit cremations because of a belief in a bodily resurrection. Some still hold to that position today, while many see Paul's words "To be absent from the body is to be present with the Lord" as an acceptable position. This avoids the resurrection debate. Whatever position the Muslim patient takes it is still a strong sign of faith in God, which is basic to their condition in the future life.

* * *

Any understanding of contemporary Islamic thought on the Resurrection and Judgment must stand on two basic Islamic doctrines—human accountability and divine justice. Concern with the eschaton is necessary to provide the stimulus to ensure present moral righteousness among the people. In this, Islamic criticism and warning against moral decadence in this generation are justified.

Chapter 9

The Place of Prayer

Much emphasis has been placed upon the second Pillar of Islam—prayer. Yet little has been written (at least in English) explaining its form and meaning. Great stress has been place upon the importance of facing Mecca when praying. Sir Muhammad Iqbal argues that the place, matter, and manner are not the most important aspects of prayer.[1] In support of this he quotes the Koran, which urges its followers not to dispute the differences in practices of sacred rites.

> For every community We have ordained a ritual which they observe. Let them not dispute you concerning this. Call them to the path of your Lord: you are rightly guided. If they argue with you, say: "God knows best all that you do. On the Day of Resurrection God will judge the differences." (S. 22:69)

> To God belongs the east and the west. Whichever way you turn there is the face of God. He is omnipotent and all knowing. (S. 2:115)

> Righteousness does not consist in whether you face towards the east or the west. The righteous man is he who believes in God on the Last Day, in the angels, and the book and the prophets; who though he dearly loves it, gives away his wealth to kinsfolk, to orphans, to the destitute, to the traveler in need and to beggars and for the redemption of captives; who attends to his prayers and renders the alms levy; who is true to his promises and steadfast in trial and in adversity and in times of war. Such are the true believers; such are the God-fearing. (S. 2:177)

Royston Pike uses this last verse to highlight the necessity of a right attitude to the prayer.[2]

The tenor of Iqbal's thesis is that prayer is instinctive in origin and is really seeking knowledge. It rises higher than thoughts to reach reality. It brings "spiritual illumination," by which the true personality is discovered in the wholeness of Life. He sees prayer demanding a concrete living experience of God as the modern mind demands a concrete existential thinking. Iqbal moves beyond the individual to state that the real object of prayer is obtained through the corporate act of worship in the congregation. He describes individual or corporate prayer as "an expression of man's inner yearning for a response in the awful silence of the Universe." In Islam there are three major types of prayer, which we need to consider. *Salat* are prayers of devotion and worship, *Shafa'a* are prayers of intercession on behalf of the dead, and *Du'a* are prayers for personal assistance in daily living.

SALAT—FORMAL/LITURGICAL PRAYERS

Salat is the core of public and private devotions. It consists in repeating it five times per day as an affirmation of the faith held. It is a period spent detached from the world. The postures are important, as they emphasize the spirits of adoration and submission. The repeating of passages from the Koran serves several purposes. These include seeking God's guidance to follow his path and thus avoid his wrath, and as a reminder of the Day of Judgment. After this time of rededication normal life is resumed. This is followed a few hours later by similarly re-presenting the self to God for similar reasons. By this faithful observance, the faithful do not lose sight of their purpose and mission in life. More frequently it is observed in this daily fashion as personal devotion. Then, on Friday, there is the general corporate call to salat.

It has been suggested that salat five times a day provides the minimum of required daily exercise. More important, it creates an awareness of our covenant with God, refreshing faith and reminding of the last days.

It has been described as being the secret to safeguarding and protecting the faith, emphasizing as it does humbleness and sur-

render to God. It provides a refuge and security for the believer.
Haneef states, "Salat is the most fundamental requirement in Islam, without which a Muslim is not fulfilling even the most basic
obligation to God and may well have lost the most important and
precious thing in life. . . ." [3]

Iqbal, in spite of the prophet's statements concerning the non-
essential nature of posture and position, justifies present Muslim
practice. He suggests that the unity of direction and movements of
the body (where all prostrate themselves) is a sign of social equality. It signifies this essential unity of humankind, destroying all
barriers.

Certain ritual washings must precede these formal prayers in order to achieve full value for the prayers. Normal Salat ablution requires the washing with water of all exposed parts of the hands and
arms to elbows, feet and ankles, the face and all facial orifices, and
the hair and head are to be rubbed with wet hands.[4]

Salat has little bearing upon the needs and stresses of a hospital
patient except for the maintenance of the personal spiritual relationship with God.

SHAFA'A—INTERCESSION FOR THE DEAD

Intercession (Shafa'a) became extremely important for the hope
of ultimate pardon. Shafa'a is intercession with the end of release
from the torment after death. It should be understood as being
available for those in Barzakh. The word intercession is used
twenty-nine times in the Koran. Its basic message is that on the
Day of Judgment it will not be available.

> Warn those who dread to be assembled before their Lord that
> they have no guardian or intercessor besides God, so that they
> may guard themselves against evil. (S. 6:51)

There are some passages that keep the door open for intercession. Sura 53:26 speaks of angels being available for intercession
only with God's permission. Other verses place true believers and
God's covenant holders as being acceptable to God as intercessors. Mohammad is asked by God to intercede on behalf of living

believers. The Hadith support Mohammed's role in this. Al Ghazali expresses confidence that all the prophets, the faithful, the learned, and the pious are appropriate intercessors on behalf of friends and relatives. Smith and Haddad concur that intercession had played and continues to play a very important role in the lives of many Muslims.

Modern writers support the idea of intercession for those who have some faith. For many, this intercession stresses God's nature as the sole authority that acts responsibly and justly in matters of punishments and remission of punishments. No intercession is possible without God's permission. Intercession proves God's mercy. However, this does not alter the fact of our own accountability. One experiences Shafa'a according to merit gained. The three unforgivable sins: murder, shirk (association of God with other Gods), and kufr (rejection of the prophet and his message) are beyond the bounds of intercession. It appears that the dominant contemporary understanding is that some form of intercession will occur on the last day, including that of Mohammed's role as intercessor.

In today's Muslim society Shafa'a is an acceptable practice of prayer (see Appendix 1). Surviving family members are expected to intercede with God and the Prophet on behalf of the deceased for the remission of afterlife punishment.

DU'A—INTERCESSION FOR THE LIVING

In observing and conversing with Muslims in the Middle East and Australia there is the practice of praying to God for specific personal and community needs. These prayers often pertain to physical and personal well-being.

The general prayer at the end of the Friday Mosque Salat is impersonal and asks God to heal the sick, lift the burden, and take away the debts of the poor. On the ninth day of the Haj every year a tent city is pitched at Mount Arafat so that the pilgrims may offer special intercessory prayers invoking God's mercy and forgiveness for themselves, their parents, and their children—including the dead. Du'a is little mentioned in literature. Personally, I found Muslims reticent to talk about it. The conjecture is that interces-

sion may be taken as a criticism or questioning of God's will and
determination for our lives. Abu Isaaq Adham gave ten reasons
why Du'as are not answered. These included items such as: failing
to fulfill duties to God; of reciting but not practicing the Koran; of
professing allegiance to God but not following traditions; of standing
alongside of Satan; of criticizing others and not self, and so on.[5] In
personal communications with a wide range of Muslims from
many stations in life, including health care workers and two Muslim High Court Judges, the consensus is that prayers for the living
and the hospitalized are desired, appreciated, and acceptable.

One High Court Judge particularly mentioned a fourth type of
Prayer, Sabr—the Prayer for Patience. It is a prayer expected and
desired in a time of crisis. It is a prayer for strength to bear the
trauma and anxiety of the current experience, which does not
mean trying to counter or avoid the consequences of God's will.

Sabr calls upon God's mercy to sustain the sufferer during the
ordeal. From this we may conclude that an essential aspect of Du'a
offered for a patient or relative will be for Sabr.

There is a need and place for prayers for the living in Islam. Many
Du'a prayers by traditional Muslims tend to be formalistically offered, thus lacking the personal element that patients inwardly
crave. Often, Du'a for Muslim patients may be appropriately offered. They also must be given the opportunity to accept or reject
such prayer offers (see Appendix 2). Discernment of the patient's
feeling concerning this must be sensitively appraised. Never should
a pastoral caregiver manipulate the patient's weakened condition
and his or her confinement to bed to force anything, including Du'a,
if they do not desire it. My experience has been that Muslims with
whom I have prayed have appreciated it. Other times, when it has
not been deemed wise to pray, the simple parting blessing, "May
God's Peace be upon you," has been gratefully received.

Chapter 10

Sunnis and Shi'as

For many in the West, the Iran and Iraqi war highlighted the sad division that exists among Muslims. In Islam, the two main factions are Sunni and Shi'a.

Let it be clearly acknowledged that there is no religion on earth in which major theological or social divergences have not brought their own divisive followers.

In Christianity the many branches of the church are well known. Christian history records many accounts of violent bloodshed and murder.

The more passive, peaceful, and nonviolent Buddhism has its various schools of thought and practice, including Mahayana and Theravada.

Hinduism has a multiplicity of gods each having their own particular class of adherents. Shiva (Shib), the Destroyer God's supporters, known as Shaivites, aim to rid their souls of bondage by ascetic practices, yoga, penance, and renunciations. The preserver god Vishnu's devotees focus upon worship, temple, and architecture and carvings as well as the family shrine.

Following the death of the Prophet in C.E. 632 the appointment of his successor as the first caliph was Abu Bakr, with Umar as the second. These two were close companions and confidants of the Prophet. Uthman became the third caliph.

A number who believed that Ali, the cousin and husband of the Prophet's favorite daughter, Fatima, should have been his successor did not approve these appointments. Ali was appointed the fourth caliph after the assassination of Uthman. There was a suspicion that Fatima and her supporters were behind the murder.

As evidence began to accumulate that this was probably the case, mistrust and anger continued to mount against Ali and Fatima. This resulted in a battle at Karbala in Iraq in C.E. 661, when Fatima, Ali, and their sons Hasan and Husayn were slain. Thus the division between the Sunnis, the followers of the first three caliphs, and the Shi'as, the proclaimers of Ali's caliphship became irreparable.

For the Shi'as the five key figures of theology and history are The Prophet, Fatima, Ali, Hasan, and Husayn. They are often symbolized by the thumb and four fingers of a hand. Because they were linked in battle for their faith, death, martyrdom, tears, and sacrifice are integral to the Shia story. Thus Shi'as are expected to respond to a call by their leadership for sacrifice. The Shi'as form a minority amongst the followers of Islam. At the time of the Karbala disaster, Ali's center of operation was in Persia, now Iran, where much of their strength still exists.

There are no major differences between the theological position of the Sunnis and Shi'as. The Five Pillars of Islam are central to both. The Supreme and Omnipotent position of Allah and the uniqueness of his messenger and Holy Prophet are fundamental to both. They equally accept the Koran as the Divine Message of Allah and its proclamations concerning death, the Barzakh, the Day of Resurrection, Hell, Paradise, and so on. Death is believed to be part of God's ordained natural process by which the earthly life, as it was lived, is brought before God for judgment. Thus life and death become inevitably associated. Death is the point at which the eternal future is determined. This life is the human opportunity to prepare for the "end."

There are some minor differences in the practice of their faith. Shi'as perform Salat (daily prayers) three times per day while Sunnis pray five times per day. Shi'as observe ten days of mourning during the month of Muhurrum each year, in memory of the events of the Karbala. (For the Shi'as this has been compared with the Christians' remembrances at Easter.) At this time Shi'as grieve, hold parades symbolizing the features of the Karbala battle, recite poems that tell stories of martyrdom, and some even flagellate their bodies.

As the theological differences are minimal, pastoral visitation can be made with equanimity. Should the question of their early history be raised, or uncomplimentary remarks be made about the other section of Islam, the caregiver should not be drawn into expressions of opinion. As you visit people who approach their faith in a different way, so you should approach the Sunni and the Shia in a similar way, with a loving, caring concern.

SECTION II:
THE PRACTICE OF CARE

Chapter 11

What Is Pastoral Care?

The majority of members in pastoral care teams in Western health care institutions are Christian except in some special units, which are run by nongovernment and non-Christian religious bodies. Occasional Rabbis, Imams, and Buddhist priests are attached to chaplaincy teams in some hospitals.

In an effort to understand what pastoral care is, a good starting point would be to look at Brister's general definition:

> Pastoral care anticipates a universal interest in all persons without distinction of race, sex, social class, age or religious condition. Care for one's neighbors should permeate all levels of life: personal, vocational, family, church and social responsibilities . . . pastoral care is Christian response to humanity's hurt.[1]

Those words "A universal interest in all persons, without distinction of race, sex, social class, age or religious condition," is pertinent to our discussion. Here Brister is plainly stating that pastoral care is nondiscriminatory. That is a general principle. Certain cultural mores must be acknowledged and observed, of course. Certain subjects are taboo among Australian Aboriginals on the basis of sex, for example; there is women's business and men's business. Likewise, when offering pastoral care to a Muslim it is on a gender basis—men to men, women to women. All cultures have differing customs that need to be respected, particularly in the hospital setting. A male chaplain may offer pastoral care to a female muslim in the presence of the patient's male relatives.

Observing special cultural norms, the pastoral care worker should always embrace the principle that pastoral care is the response of the caregiver to anyone who is hurting. When such care is made available to a Muslim patient, that aim is to assist the patient and family to work through the crisis of hospitalization in such a way that would be applauded by Jesus, who set the example for pastoral care with the following parable.

In a remote village in Indian tiger country a young calf strayed from the village herd during the day. The search up until nightfall proved futile. About 3 a.m., the man of the household was so concerned that, at great inconvenience, he rose and with a lantern went into the jungle calling for that calf. He was taking a risk of either tiger or leopard attack upon himself. After a while his calling brought a response from the terrified calf. Putting it across his shoulders he carried it back to its relieved mother. Jesus' parable was of the hundredth sheep that was lost and searched for until found. For the Christian pastoral caregiver, that is the motivation required. Wherever a person is bewildered, confused, frightened, in pain, depressed, and worried in the hospital, whether Christian, Muslim, Hindu, Jew, or no faith at all, that person is hurting and in need of help.

A surgical patient indicated her religion as Jewish. On my first visit I clearly sensed a negative attitude toward a visit from a member of the clergy. She gave two blatant, glaring "keep away" signals: She asked me to call a nurse to bring an analgesic; then to make certain, she added, "and a bed pan." Sensing she was a troubled lady, I cheerily visited the next day as if nothing had happened. Visits were made each day until she was discharged. Her designated religion was a misnomer. She opened up and told her story of a life of prostitution in a world-famous red-light district. During her hospitalization many of her issues were aired. We didn't talk of religion. On the morning of her discharge she was affectionately, even embarrassingly, profuse in her thanks for my being a friend to her.

Pastoral care requires making an effort to connect personally with people in need. Many hurting people do not display a placard saying, "Help Me." My surgical patient initially was trying to avoid a religious person. The caregiver needs to be sensitively perceptive, even from the first encounter, of the possibility of factors—medical, social, or otherwise—affecting the patient or the relatives.

Jesus told the story of the rebellious son who left home and lived a less than honorable life. He sank to live among the dregs of human society. Yet his father never gave up hope of his return. The father in the story is God. God never gives up on his wayward children. No one should be beyond our willingness to make a real effort toward support and care.

Jesus, the Jew, also told the story of a pathetic Jewish traveler who was robbed, beaten, and left for dead on the treacherous Jericho road. He was given first aid and cared for by a religiously despised Samaritan. Similarly the Christian, who is considered by many Muslims to be an infidel, is authorized to stretch out the hand of love, mercy, and compassion to all, including our Muslim brother, sister, or neighbor. How can we interpret it otherwise? Jesus was demonstrating a secondary issue beyond the question of "Who is my neighbor?" He was denoting the nature of true pastoral care.

The assaulted traveler was a person in need. Physical need certainly was evident, as well as other pressing anxieties. He was robbed of his traveling money and goods. Perhaps he had been to Jerusalem to sell crafts or produce to sustain him and his family. Now all was gone. We are not certain of the nature of the business his journey involved. Did the mugging undo the purpose of the excursion from home? He required treatment for his injuries. From where would he get the resources to pay for it away from home? Lying on the road helpless and bleeding, he became a spectacle for ghoulish passers-by such as the priest and the Levite. He was deeply humiliated and his self-esteem was shattered. Anger, resentment, distrust, and other negative emotional and psychological reactions were stewing in his mind.

Along came a man upon whom he would normally spit. Without a second thought, this Samaritan ministered pastoral care to him. The bathing of the wounds, the ride on the ass to Jericho, the accommodation at the inn, the additional treatment and feeding costs until he was well were included in the care. Jesus had no need to continue the parable. The lesson was obvious. Pastoral care as Brister defined it is to be offered to all, irrespective of age, gender, color, race, or religion. During the remaining miles to Jericho we can only speculate. No doubt the Samaritan offered many words of encouragement and continued support. Efforts to relieve the anxiety and stress created by the vicious attack would have been made. Arrival and accommodation at the inn must have seemed like entering Paradise.

Inevitably, after receiving such care from this stranger and during the remainder of the journey to Jericho a mutually positive relationship must have developed between this odd couple—a Jew and a Samaritan. When genuine pastoral care is offered and accepted, it develops a mutual sharing, one with the other. The victim in the story needed to relate his feelings to the caregiver. The remembered details, the suddenness of the attack, the brutality, the outnumbering, the helplessness, how the wounds were afflicted, and the concern for his family are but some of the aspects of the intimacy shared along the way.

The caregiver's listening ear with its encouraging empathy helps to empty the dam of pent-up emotions. The caregiver's only interruptions are to maintain the wounded's awareness that his or her words are being heard. Very occasionally there may be a brief interjection to share a personal episode in order to reinforce the empathy being shown. It must be remembered that no two people react or experience the same or similar events identically. Thus the caregiver is building up a helpful rapport with the patient. I have often been amazed at the depth of the intimacy of the relationship built up within an hour between myself as a chaplain and the family of a traumatized patient in the accident emergency unit where a loved one is fighting for life or been sent to the operating room for life-saving emergency surgery. Such relationships are enriching and positively helpful for all. Thus pastoral care develops the type of sustaining relationship the family needs at that time.

Jesus' parable stresses the nature of nondiscriminatory pastoral care. A Muslim may offer true pastoral care to a Christian, a Hindu to a Christian, and a Buddhist to a Christian or vice versa. Where need exists, whoever is in the position and has the spiritual sensitivity is obligated to offer unconditional pastoral care. Christians should not consider themselves to be the only persons with a "caring spirit." Many from other religions also display an awareness of the need to support and provide for others in need. The Muslim observance of Zakat (almsgiving) keeps alive the concept of caring for others. The Red Crescent, the Muslim equivalent to the Red Cross is another example.

In a hospital, large or small, pastoral caregivers should have a Jericho-road outlook to make themselves available as caring people, whoever the patient may be. Put into the context of the twenty-first century situation of the West Bank in Israel, the victim on the road might be a Jew who had been attacked by extremists, and a Muslim would be helping the Jew. This is the picture of care that Jesus was presenting in the parable about neighbors. In this generation of the global village all, irrespective of age, gender, color, race, or religion are our neighbors. Any one of them may require, let me stress, *unconditional* pastoral care.

Clebsch and Jaekle, in their classic book *Pastoral Care in Historical Perspective,* offer a definition of pastoral care: "The ministry of the cure of souls or pastoral care consists of helping acts done by representative Christian persons, directed toward healing, sustaining, guiding and reconciling of persons whose trouble arises in the context of ultimate meanings and concerns."[2]

Clebsch and Jaekle readily admit that the four special functions mentioned in their definition may not all be used in every case. They perceive pastoral care adapting itself to the prevailing circumstances. Often it is not possible to facilitate reconciliation with God for any number of reasons. It may require the utilization of the patient's present spiritual enlightenment to lead to reconciliation with a God of whom we have insufficient knowledge. Others may recall earlier experiences with religion or life which have left a negative attitude toward God. If the caregiver is the right person at the right time, he or she may be able to effect the patient's reconciliation with God. Again, pastoral care offered and received may pave the way for reconciliation later by someone else.

Clebsch and Jaekle state, "Christian Pastoring is a helping act performed by persons who represent the resources of wisdom and authority of Christianity in one or other of its versions." This does not necessarily imply spiritual direction or pastoral counseling. Acts such as touch, presence, words of comfort, counsel, plain interest and concern, or spiritual direction are able to bring forth a response from the patient if the representative concept fully permeates the relationship. By being a caring representative of Christ (without the strings of imperialistic missionary days), the arms of companionship and friendship are extended to Muslims. By this, any existing spirit of antipathy, suspicion, or antagonism is softened and a spirit of appreciation of each other is gained.

Some would question whether this was Christian pastoral care. If the ministry is to non-Christians then it is largely a healing and sustaining encounter. In the hospital setting the medical processes of healing are in the hands of the medical professionals. What is demanded from the chaplain is a healing or calming of the patient's spirit or mind so that the medical procedures may be more effective. The healing is directed toward the traumas, mental torments, fears, and apprehensions, as well as the isolation that hospitalization brings. Most hospital patients, of whatever cultural or religious background, carry such baggage. They are removed from home, family, and familiar surroundings into a clinical atmosphere. In addition, there come "superior" professional figures standing over them pronouncing diagnoses, treatments, various probable side effects, and outcomes—often "scary stuff."

The caregiver approaches to the patient to heal, tame, or soothe the rampaging fears, exaggerations and, more seriously, the denials of the situation as perceived by the patient. The medical staff's treatment, whether it be medication or surgery, is rendered less effective while such negative thoughts thrive and fester. In this sense, pastoral care plays a healing role to those of any or no faith. For the Muslim, the fact that the same God of Abraham, Isaac, and Jacob motivates the caregiver puts the care into perspective for them.

The role as a sustainer is to maintain an evenness of mental temperament as each stage of the hospitalization unfolds. Working in a hematology unit for many years the need for this sustaining ministry was obvious. Response to chemotherapy may be a remission gained early but a relapse some time later. Further remissions and relapses may follow. Each time a relapse occurs, the shortness of time with loved ones and life becomes more of a reality. The issues of unfinished business concerning home, family, and career become overpowering and disturbing. The personal spirituality, training, and skills of the caregiver are increasingly stretched. Dependence upon God for wisdom to sustain some meaning and ultimate hope in the life of the patient becomes more difficult and important. To leave the patient lying on the road is not Jesus' perception of pastoral care. Here the turning of the mind to God, if possible, is paramount so that the patient may experience God's peace in what, possibly, are terminal days. At such times encounters with the patient must be without personal religious agendas and set theological processes for attaining reconciliation. The heavy imposition of spiritual pressure on the patient may cause additional excessive pain, displeasure, and antagonism.

Earlier in the chapter it was suggested that we should use the patients present spiritual enlightenment to seek reconciliation with God. In all religions, the average believer's God is far too small. I believe that God is able to meet each person at individual levels of spirituality as he or she calls out to God in the hour of crisis. Here the words of Jesus are relevant, "Seek and you shall find, ask and you shall receive, and knock and it shall be opened to you" (Luke 11:9 *NIV*). Here, let it be clear, only one God will always respond to the sincere call of one of his creatures. Countless have been the times I have been with a dying patient of seemingly poor spiritual sensitivity (rather than unreligious). In the preceding days, the individual had not wished to face the reality of the closeness of life's earthly journey; and the so-called reconciling ministry seemed impossible. This simple prayer, uttered even when a patient is comatose, has proved effective: "May your spirit be lifted up to God, whose spirit is reaching down to you, and whose peace overflows you and unites you with Him." Before this prayer was completed, many times the patient had departed this life with a smile on his or her face.

One memorable case was that of a former prisoner of war in the notorious Japanese Changi camp in Singapore. On his return home he found it difficult to show, receive, or give love. For forty years he had not spoken to most of his nine children, after he abandoned their mother on his return to Australia. Now, riddled with cancer, he lay in a coma in an intensive care unit. His two youngest daughters, who had been caring for him, were each holding one of his hands as I prayed such a prayer to this agnostic/atheistic, unloving father. Tears were in their eyes as I finished. Their father had squeezed their hands simultaneously during the prayer. For them it was the first sign of affection he had displayed to them in all their life. They were infants when he went to war. Half an hour later the nursing staff and myself were astonished to see this man sit up, stretch out his hands with a huge smile on his face, then lie back to take his last breath. I believe that was reconciliation without theological prescriptions.

Pastoral care may be seen as springing out of a genuine concern for other people's well-being. Such caring can be performed by anyone. Christian pastoral care has something over other types of care in that it has a Christian dimension. It becomes Christian when Christians, sustained by Christian faith, exercise it. They also are activated by a personal experience between themselves and God. Their care is practiced in the pattern and spirit set by Jesus in his life and teachings. Thus inspired by the spirit of Christ, it becomes Christlike.

The relationship of the Christian caregiver is able to offer an additional element through the divine relationship between the caregiver and God. This is my definition of Christian pastoral care:

> Christian pastoral care is entering into a concerned, caring relationship with a person in need by one who is effectually motivated by a personal relationship with God through Jesus. Christian pastoral care is a Christian's loving interest and compassion for what matters most for the other's good, whoever that person might be.

Pastoral care becomes Christian when it is exercised by Christians who are sustained by the Christian faith and activated by the personal experience between the caregiver and God. The care may not be different in method from another's caring work. Someone has said that it is exercised with the gentle, confident, encouraging touch of Jesus seen in the person of the caregiver.

Campbell[3] and Taylor[4] see Christian care in the environment of mutuality. It is in a spirit of companionship with the patient that their needs and anxieties may be faced. In the Jericho-road story, the socially unacceptable Samaritan became the companion of the robbery victim. He dismounted, knelt down, treated his wounds, lifted him upon his ass, and then walked beside him the many miles to Jericho. It again reminds us of the description of Jesus as the Good Shepherd, who goes out looking for the lost sheep. The parallel between the Samaritan and the shepherd is significant for our understanding of mutuality in pastoral care.

Although chaplains should conduct themselves as professionals working among other professionals, there is also a need to be the lowly companion. The lowly person sheds the aura of the trained expert and the knowledgeable one while practicing his or her professional skills. The chaplain becomes the one alongside—eyelevel to eyelevel. The towering, haughty hospital professional stands looking down at the helpless, captive, prostrate patient in bed. The Christian caregiver is seen only as a friend holding and supporting the incapacitated along his or her painful, uncertain journey.

The Samaritan, the disrespected outsider, was like that shepherd. Any shepherd 2,000 years ago in Palestine was so inferior that his testimony in a law court was considered unreliable and thus was dismissed. A fellow traveler treading the same bumpy, dusty road of life is the caregiver who comes to the hospitalized—one to whom the patient is able to respond. Jesus uses verbal brushes to paint the picture of the caregiver as one who considers himself or herself to be an equal to the one needing the care. By this the doors of mutuality of sharing swing open. Confidence is established. Communication flows. Encouragement is realized. Henri Nouwen described the chaplain as the "wounded healer." Heiji Faber saw the image as that of a "clown in the circus." Both are human, earthly pictures of the chaplain. These are the types that patients, whether Christian, Muslim, Jewish, Hindu, Buddhist, agnostic, or atheist, would prefer to see beside them in hospital.

On many occasions there are no chairs available or other visitors are occupying them. In order to emphasize the companionship and closeness, I have knelt at the bedside, holding the patient's hand so that our faces have been on the same level.

In such a ministry to Muslims our motivation is that of mutuality and companionship, leading to improved psychological, physical, emotional, and spiritual health. Spiritual health must include sincerity in endeavoring to make an Imam available according to the patient's wishes.

Recall and reflect upon the implication of our definition of pastoral care as it would relate to your drawing alongside a Muslim patient.

In my more than forty years of full-time ministry, before retiring, for eighteen years I had been daily at the bedside of the dying, the traumatized, the recovering, the depressed, the fearful, the heartbroken, the relieved, the uncertain, the guilt-ridden, the lonely, and the rejoicing. Prior to that I had spent seventeen years on the Indian subcontinent working among lovable semiliterate villagers, meeting smart, intelligent, young future leaders, and sharing meals with those from many differing faiths. For two years I sat in refugees' quarters, eating and sleeping with them under all sorts of conditions as we planned and implemented relief and rehabilitation strategies. Our distribution of supplies was to all—Hindus, Christians, Buddhists, Animists, and whoever. Those two years, together with my service at bedsides offering pastoral care, I count as among my most enriching times. They were times when my love for my fellow human beings, whatever their color, race, gender, or faith did not matter. During these experiences, my own personal knowledge and relationship with God grew and the depth of my faith in a God who loves and cares for all his human creation became more firmly based. These were but some of the fruits of attempting to be the Samaritan on the Jericho road.

Your offering of pastoral care to a Muslim, as we have outlined, will enhance your faith, confirm the faith of the patient, and promote a spirit of peace and acceptance among people who worship the God of Abraham.

Chapter 12

Imperatives for Muslim Care

To develop long-term multicultural relationships, some basic principles need to be remembered and followed. When associating with Hindus you would not mistreat or condone the mistreatment of cows. When in the presence of a Jain, to avoid shock and deep hurt, you would gently lift the ant crawling on you and carefully place it on a leaf or other safe object. Illustrations such as these are numerous. What, then, should we do or not do when developing a friendship of mutual respect with a Muslim?

Dr. Ray Register worked for thirty years among Muslims in the Middle East. He spent much time making real friends with his Muslim neighbors. During my stay with him I met many of them and appreciated the depth of their relationships with him. Dr. Register gives us seven basic principles to remember and follow in our dialoguing with Muslims. We are able to apply them to our caring for Muslims in the hospital environment.

1. The Muslim is generally an easy person to know.
2. Learn as much as possible about the culture and its religious emphasis.
3. Treat the Bible and the Koran with respect.
4. Normally the use of important Christian terms such as "Son of God," "Lord" (to be used as an ascription to God alone, not Jesus), and "Trinity" should be avoided.
5. Deal with Muslims of your own gender.
6. The building of a relationship is important.
7. A Muslim will not expect you to be an expert in the Koran.

If the Muslim was born overseas and in particular is from a Muslim-majority country he or she often exhibits a keenness to associate with the locals and learn as much as possible about the new country and thus make the friendships needed. There is a desire to be accepted and to belong. Often the host country's citizens maintain an air of superiority because the newcomers are not Christians. To find an accepting Christian is sometimes looked upon as a bonus.

True friendship is shown in our desire to learn as much about Islam as possible, both its cultural differences and its religious differences. In doing so, do not approach such new insights from the old colonialist missionary practice of trying to find the negatives. As we have seen, Islam is loaded with positives and similarities to Christianity. Focus upon and accept the positives. Look for the positives. That is the way to friendship.

Muslims revere their scriptures—the Koran and the Hadith. They also respect the revelations of God given through the Jewish prophets and Jesus. The scriptures are the "Word of God." To write in or underline any scripture is to deface that sacred revelation. A Muslim would see your marked Bible or Koran as being sacrilegious. You would lose respect as a godly person or you would not be seen as a representative of God.

For the Muslim the monotheistic stance is the very basis of their faith. Mohammed was vehement on this issue and much of the crusading zeal of early Islam was based upon eliminating polytheism from the earth. Register warns about words that imply that Jesus is God. The Muslims see Jesus as being a god alongside of Allah. To them the Trinity suggests three gods, of which the Holy Spirit is the third. For the Muslim, this is also the grossest blasphemy. In referring to Jesus, he is to the Muslim the "Word of God," "The Messiah" or "Anointed One," and the "One born of the Spirit." A Muslim's conception of the role of the Messiah may vary from the Christian and the Jewish interpretation. Avoid offensive arguments and debates, which will do nothing to advance friendship with your Muslim acquaintance.

The relationship will prosper only if it is built upon a foundation of trust. That trust matures as your new friend sees that he or she can rely upon you to keep whatever is said between you in the strictest confidence. The Muslim extended family allows for the minimum of personal privacy. The family, its promotion, and unity make a strong obligatory demand upon the individual. There are matters that a Muslim keeps pent up inside because he or she fears family reaction if such thoughts were voiced. There is a possibility that, if there is sufficient confidence in your trustworthiness, some deeper sharing may take place.

Quoting the Koran as a means of building the Muslim's respect for you could have negative results. Read and study the Koran thoroughly before making detailed citations. Muslims are appreciative of your interest and do not expect you to be knowledgeable in their scriptures.

With these fundamental principles firmly in our minds it is time for us to look at the ways we can effectively care for a Muslim patient.

Chapter 13

Beside the Patient

Feeling nervous? Your hospital ward list has a patient registered as a Muslim. Perhaps you have avoided them before. They believe so differently from us about God. Western media report some unpleasant things about Muslims in the Middle East. In Muslim countries negative reports about Christians in the West are featured in their media.

You are a pastoral caregiver and have been commissioned by your church and accepted by the Pastoral Care Department of the hospital to minister to patients. You even may be able to help this patient with more issues than the patient you are more comfortable visiting. Any pastoral visit requires you to have a sense of dependence upon God to give you the words and wisdom to most effectively lift with the tender hands of a shepherd this member of the flock of God. By using your pastoral gift with this patient, you will be declaring and demonstrating that the mercy and compassion of God are not restricted to one group of people.

Here we will look at eight caring principles that you may use in your relationship with this patient.

ACCEPTANCE

First, it is important to remember that you are meeting with a person from a different culture, different ethnic background, different religious beliefs and practices, and with different needs. Habits and attitudes will be contrary to your upbringing. Perhaps statements will be made which may sound sacrilegious to you.

Occasions will occur when you will find it difficult to conceive how some thoughts or actions could logically be entertained. Remember the Muslim is probably thinking the same about you. As a caring person you must be in control of yourself. The slightest verbal or nonverbal indication of repulsion or disapproval may negate any mutuality that has been established. The first criterion of any care for Muslims must be an acceptance of them and their ways without qualification. Our cultural ways are important to us and only changeable under certain circumstances. Similarly, the Muslim way of life is vital and important to them. You will find that Arab Muslims will differ in some respects from Pakistani, Bengali, Egyptian, or Indonesian Muslims. You must be willing to accept them as they are with all their differences. Continuing to maintain a warm interest in and a concern for them is, essentially, the first necessity toward building a caring relationship.

Acceptance must be genuine and sincere. Your early encounters are inevitably treated with suspicion. The motive for a nonbeliever (a Christian) to take an interest in them will be thought to be ulterior and evangelical. Your Muslim contact will have to be satisfied that your interest in him or her is without strings and real. As the Samaritan neighbor's motive was purely to provide the best care for the victim without thought of proselytizing, so we must give care without ulterior motive. As well as supporting the patient in his or her need, the intention is the building of multicultural bridges, not scoring religious points for your own faith. If our caring breaks down animosity and promotes an acceptance of one another and a respect of our differences, then the Samaritan role is being fulfilled.

Unless you are able to accept them as sincerely as Jesus so outrageously (in Jewish eyes) accepted Matthew, Zacchaeus, the woman of Samara, or the woman taken in adultery, all efforts to minister to a Muslim will be futile. In such cases, the caregiver is the one likely to be rejected or else used and manipulated.

AVAILABILITY

In the East, time is of lesser consequence than in Western society. A Muslim (who is often of Asian-continental origin), likes attention and particularly people who will spend time sitting and talking with him or her. That desire for attention is heightened when the person has a physical ailment. You will need to be available to spend time with the patient and the family. Constant clock watching will be perceived as a lack of true caring. They interpret this as a sign that you are only doing it for what you can get out of it for yourself or your religion. An unhurried willingness to be available for the Muslim will open the door to a mutual acceptance and trust.

If you are to be available it may mean a reorganization of your visitation priorities. The temptation will be to take the easier way out and concentrate on the easier, less-needy, and well-cared-for regular Christian parishioners.

In my own chaplaincy ministry my top priority was for the less religious and less pastorally cared-for patients. The person who had a regular stream of denominational visitors did not really require a chaplain's visit unless particular medical circumstances required a more professional knowledge of hospital protocol, the course of the disease, its treatment, and its effects on the patient. Involvement in clinical meetings considerably aided in understanding the special needs of particular patients. Such knowledge was not available to the casual pastoral visitor.

The extra time spent with the Muslim patient might require a little longer stay at the hospital in order to catch up on some other patients. Availability is the hallmark of a good pastoral worker.

GREETING

The first words of greeting are important to Muslims. It gives them an immediate understanding of where you stand. Be prepared to greet the Muslim with the words, "Salaam Ali Kum" (May God's peace be with you). Then wait for the response, "Ali Kum Salaam." If you are greeted first then you must offer the response. This mutual use of God's name puts you on common ground. It has a deeper significance than the Jewish greeting of "shalom" (peace). As Christians we have lost the early Christian practice of meeting with a "peace" greeting.

Confidence may be further gained when the word "Bishmi'llah" (In the name of God) is appropriately used. This is particularly so when used in the context of some prayer, blessing, or action for the benefit of the patients or relatives. It brings God into relevant position in the relationship. It encourages the confidence and trust desired in the visit. A prayer may be concluded with the utterance of this word.

The recognition of God is important for the Muslim. In the hospital scene the need is important for the mercy and compassion of God to be invoked upon the life of the patient and family. The initial greeting seeking God's peace will get you off to an encouraging start.

INITIATING CONVERSATION

We have already suggested that a Muslim is easy to get to know. A Muslim loves to talk, as do most people who come from the Middle East and the rest of Asia. Your ability to elicit free-flowing conversation endears you to them.

Topics that will spark their interest are those that generate talk of their homeland, their family, and their religion. Lebanese Muslims delight in conversing about their famous cedars, their mountains, and their fruit orchards in Lebanon or their local village or town. Indonesian Muslims will speak of their tropical islands and surrounding waters. A Pakistani Muslim man will be difficult to stop if the topic of cricket is raised. The African may wax eloquent about the desert sands or the wild animals of his or her homeland. Turkish Muslims will recall their history, including the Ottoman's Blue Mosque or the whirling dervishes. For the Muslim there is much to talk about.

Revealing a smattering of knowledge concerning Islam and expressing the desire to know more will help to minimize any suspicions that they may have concerning your motivation and interest in them. To talk of God's power, the future life (if appropriate), the history of Mohammed's life and the history of Islam will open the floodgates of conversation.

Standing in an airline queue, a Westernized Bengali Muslim businesswoman, who also was the wife of a top Bengali bureaucrat, engaged me in conversation. She suggested that we book adjoining plane seats. For the next ninety minutes before the plane flight and the hour in the plane to Calcutta we had a nonstop conversation. She told me of her career, of her husband, of his important work, and especially we shared something of our personal experiences of God. There was a deep sense of God's presence and inspiration in that encounter. Although this ran contrary to normal gender contacts, her social contacts in diplomatic circles had broken the strict Muslim code. It does demonstrate the Muslim willingness to converse with those outside their culture. In the hospital, the practice of same-gender visits should be strictly observed.

CONVERSATIONS INVOLVING RELIGION

It is very easy for a Christian to have a sense of superiority in religious perception. We have been conditioned to think of all non-Christians as heathens or pagans. Most Christians believe that Christ is the only way to God. Similarly, the Muslim considers all non-Muslims as infidels who, in the teaching of the traditions, should be put to the sword. The meeting between two religiously intolerant groups could be explosive. Your inquiry concerning Islam should involve openness in sharing, gaining knowledge and understanding of what your new friend believes. Ascertaining such background will help you to avoid inflammatory confrontation by unintentionally offensive remarks. Your Muslim companion will make comments, that may seem offensive to you concerning your own Christian beliefs. Remember that you may be harboring, if not expressing, offensive thoughts concerning Islam. Your readiness not to rise to a defensive and therefore antagonistic stance will help keep communication lines open. Your friend, like you, has a misinformed and biased version of what the other believes. Heated, defensive, offending debate will shatter any rapport that is being established. It is probable that both of you have some but not all of the truth on your side. We must admit to a mutual ignorance in many matters of each other's beliefs.

A wise philosophy is that there is no need for any of us to defend God. God is big enough to defend himself. The best form of redress for any hurt is for both of you to let your own knowledge of

God and his spirit and mind within you, shine forth as a love and a desire for understanding to be experienced between you.

LISTENING

In your pastoral care or counseling training the art of listening has been emphasized and reemphasized. It will remain one of the best therapeutic tools. This applies even more so to our Muslim friends. When they get started they are good conversationalists. In conversation the caregiver should do little talking. When you are a skilled listener you do not engage yourself with a patient or a family with your own agenda or a lot of probing, personal questions. You allow the other person to provide the lead once the conversation begins to flow. They are expressing their concerns as they converse. When troubled, they will likely reveal this as they talk. You may seize the odd moment to say something significant to their theme or to confirm that you are following their words. What may be viewed as the lesser role is, in fact, more important because it is building the patient's confidence in you. By expressing themselves openly patients become more accepting of you and tolerant of what you may throw into the conversation.

As the encounter is in a hospital setting, the listening ear allows the patient or family to voice feelings about what is happening as a result of the illness or accident. This only occurs after a degree of intimacy has developed in the relationship. It is in this listening that emotions are able to find expression. The measure of Muslim concept of your empathy may be seen when they begin to share deeper feelings. It is through this that the pastoral caregiver is able to make available the type of support and counsel that is needed. This becomes therapeutic for patients emotionally, physically, and spiritually.

PRAYER

The spiritual positives are able to go even farther when the suitable moment arrives to offer prayer. It may not arise in some cases and if it does not, there is no need to feel that your visit has failed.

In most cases, a Muslim will cling to the words that would be offered to God for peace, healing, strength, mercy, and forgiveness to flow from God to the patient and family. If you are a male and the patient is female a prayer should be made in the presence of a male member of the patient's family with whom you have developed a friendship. The male caregiver should not touch the female patient during the prayer.

At the beginning or the end of the prayer the word "Bishmi'llah" (in the name of Allah) may be used with positive acceptance. In offering a prayer (Du'a) of intercession you are fulfilling what is usually the deepest desire of a Muslim in those circumstances. Although some workers among Muslims pray in the name of Jesus, I consider it wiser to avoid offense and pray using the name of God or Allah.

Prayers using the normal Christian phrases and distinctives should be avoided. Such usage may be misunderstood as an effort to evangelize. Remember you are there to provide practical pastoral care to an ailing person and his or her family. Thus any thought of proselytizing while the patient and family are experiencing the crisis of hospitalization should not be considered. This applies during prayer and must be scrupulously recognized. Such an infringement would rob the patient and family of any efficacy that might be experienced by the prayer and your visit. Your prayer should be helpful, meaningful, and express the thoughts that the patient and family would pray themselves. Such a perceptive prayer can only be uttered as a result of your acceptance of the patient and family. Your unhurried availability and listening ear is then able to distill into the right type of prayer your insights into the family's need.

VISITING THE HOME

If the family invites you to their home, accept the invitation. Not only is it the courteous thing to do, it also gives evidence that you are sincere in your desire to be a friend. It proves that you are a genuinely caring person. In the hospital you are more or less meeting the family on your territory. At the hospital they are the guests. You are the host. The situation is reversed when you visit their home. They are able to be more natural. They have the opportunity to share their typical cultural hospitality. This gives them scope to express their appreciation of the care you have shown toward them.

If the patient has died, then it would be a mark of respect for you to visit the home after 5 or 6 p.m. during the first week after the death. Muslim, particularly Arab, practice is for friends and relatives to pay their respects at that time. A very important and wealthy person in the Middle East is likely to have a large tent-like structure fitted out with carpets and lined with chairs. Here the chief mourners will sit at the head while the visitors come and pay their respects. For the average person this takes place in the home. The men assemble in one section of the house and the women in another. Unless a man is related or very close to the family, he should not venture near the women.

When you are shown into the room the normal greeting is given, plus a prayer-like statement such as "May . . . [Name] know the mercy and forgiveness of God in Paradise." You then take your seat silently. A small cup of black bitter coffee is brought, which you drink immediately and hand the cup back. The drinking of the coffee symbolizes the fact that you are sharing the bitterness of death with the family. There is no need for talk. One sits for at least half an hour, usually in silence, with only an occasional remark. You are then able to excuse yourself and leave. Such a visit is considered an indication of true friendship and caring concern. The family deeply values it and it is noted.

ACCEPTING THE CHALLENGE

As you look down the ward list, that designation—"Muslim"—now will leap out at you. In the past you have been able to ignore it. You have shrugged your shoulders, thinking, "This patient is not a Christian," or " I don't know anything about Muslims," or "They are not my responsibility," or "They have their own people," or even " I can't get through my visitations as it is."

You are a member of the pastoral care team of the hospital. True pastoral care offers ministry irrespective of age, color, class, culture, or religion. A hospital chaplain, in Jesus' terms, is walking the Jericho road down hospital wards where lay the sick and the wounded. The pastoral worker is the shepherd stalking through the undergrowth of a hospital searching for the lost sheep needing to be picked up and lifted back to peaceful meadows. Muslims are also among the wounded and the bewildered, lost in the world of human suffering. Although it is easier to plead ignorance of their religion and culture, it is our calling to minister to their needs.

It will be much more rewarding to experience the accepting warmth of appreciation from these people. Do not opt out of our Christian responsibility to serve these, our neighbors. For as Jesus has said, "Whatever you did for one of the least of these brothers of mine, you did it for me."

Appendix 1

Shafa'a—Prayer for the Dead

"In the following prayer recited in contemporary Egypt on the occasion of a child's death one finds a summary of the best Islamic thought concerning hope for the little one as well as comfort for those who must face the ordeal of loss."[1]

> O God, he is Thy servant and the son of Thy servant. Thou didst create him and sustain him and bring him to death and thou wilt give him life. O God make him for his parents an anticipation, riches sent before, a reward, which precedes, and through him make heavy the balance (of their good works) and increase their rewards. Let neither us nor them be seduced by temptation after his departure. O God cause him to overtake the believers who preceded him, in the guardianship of Abraham, and give him in exchange (for his earthly home) a better dwelling place and a family better than his family, and keep him sound from the temptation of the tomb and the Fire of Gehenna.[2]

Appendix 2

Bedside Prayers

DU'A—INTERCESSION FOR THE LIVING

Merciful and Compassionate God we bow before you, in full submission. The weakness in body, mind, and spirit is filling . . . [name]* with dread. You have planned our days before we were born. You are the only God. Beside you there is no other God. In your mercy look upon . . . [name] in his/her present condition. There is pain and other anxieties. The days of his/her life seem numbered. We bring . . . [name] before you that you might exercise your great compassion on him/her. Ease her pain. Give him/her strength for each day's need. We ask this so that his/her mind will not be filled with problems of his/her body but will be concentrated upon you.

May his/her thoughts be focused upon you as one who is in Islam. Keep him/her obedient to your will at all times so that on the Day . . . [name] will walk in the Garden. In the name of God— "Bishmi'llah."

* * *

All Wise, All-Knowing, Eternal God, You understand and know all that . . . [name] is experiencing in these days of illness. His/her mind is so troubled that he/she may have displeased you. Look favorably upon him/her in this hour of illness and pain. We pray that

---

*The use of the patient's name in the prayer personalizes the petition and brings greater comfort to the patient.

you will relieve . . . [name] of pain and stress. Fill . . . [name] with the calmness that your peace can give to a person's spirit. All-knowing God, we beseech you to forgive and bless him/her as he/she lies here committing his/her life into your control. Forgive, restore your peace and grant . . . [name] a safe passage across the bridge on the Day of Resurrection. In the name of God and according to your will—Insha'llah.

SABR—PRAYER FOR PATIENCE

You are the All-Powerful, Benevolent God. We come before you not with confidence in ourselves but with full trust in you. You are the All-Wise One who created. . . [name], who is before us in pain of body, distress of mind, and fearful in spirit. His/her illness is taking its toll upon him/her. We ask, Oh! Holy One, that you will be pleased to give him/her patience to endure the pain in thankfulness to you. May strength to cope with each day's burdens be granted him/her. We ask this not for ourselves but that his/her faith in you and submission to your will may not falter. Grant that faith will be sufficient unto the day when you summon all before the Judgment. On that Day may he/she be granted entry to Paradise.
Insha'llah—In the will of God.

BEDSIDE PRAYER FOR THE DYING

There is no God but Allah, the Forbearing, the Generous.
There is no God but Allah, the High, the Grand.
Praise be to Allah, the Lord of the Seven Heavens and the
Seven Earths and what is in them, between them, and
beneath them. And the Lord of the great Throne, and praise
belongs to God, the Lord of the Universe.

When death is imminent, the dying person should be made to lie facing the Qiblah (Mecca) and should recite the following prayer:

O Allah, forgive me, have mercy on me and unite me
with the Most High Companion.

The patient should also recite:

> None is worthy of praise beside Allah. Surely death has many hardships and difficulties.

The patient's prayer should continue:

> O Allah, help me in overcoming the throes and difficulties of death.

When the patient has breathed his or her last breath, the people present should close their eyes and recite the following prayer:

> O Allah, forgive . . . (name of deceased); and raise his/her status (in Jannah—the Garden) among the rightly guided people; and be his/her representative among his/her people whom he/she has left behind; and forgive us and him/her. O Sustainer of the worlds. And (O Allah) make his grave vast and accommodating and fill it with light (noor).

Contributed by the Islamic Council of NSW

Notes

Chapter 1

1. Armstrong, Karen. *History of God* (Ventura: London) 1999, p. 297.
2. Smith, Jane I. and Y.Y. Haddad, *The Islamic Understanding of Death and Resurrection* (Albany: State University of New York Press) 1981, p. 68.
3. Haneef, Suzanne. *What Everybody Should Know About Islam and Muslims* (Chicago: Kazi) 1979, p. 184.
4. Ibid.

Chapter 2

1. Haneef, Suzanne. *What Everybody Should Know About Islam and Muslims* (Chicago: Kazi) 1979, p. 3.
2. Often translated "Allah—the Greatest." This may be interpreted by English readers as "Allah is the greatest among many Gods." This concept is contrary to the Islamic Creed, hence "Allah the Almighty One" is preferred here. The Boxer, Mohammed Ali, claiming to be "the greatest" supports this.
3. Khan, Qamaruddin. "The Qu'ran and the Signs of God" in *Rabetat al –Al—al Islam,* Vol. 5, No. 10, 1978, p.10.
4. Maudidi Abu A'la. *Toward Understanding Islam* (Beirut: Holy Koran Publishing House) 1980, pp. 86-103.
5. Haneef, *What Everybody Should Know,* p. 5.
6. Ibid., p. 87.
7. Ibid., p. 65.
8. Smith, Jane I. and Y.Y. Haddad. *The Islamic Understanding of Death and Resurrection* (Albany: State University of New York Press) 1981, p. 49.
9. Ansari, F.R. *Philosophy of Worship in Islam* (Karachi: World Federation of Islamic Missions) 1964, pp. 13-14.

Chapter 3

1. Haneef, Suzanne. *What Everybody Should Know About Islam and Muslims* (Chicago: Kazi) 1979, pp. 36-37.

2. Ibid., p. 106.

3. Fisher, Mary Pat. *Living Religions* (Englewood Cliffs, NJ: Prentice-Hall) 1994, p. 312.

4. Ibid., p. 316.

5. McKane, William. *Al-Ghazali's Book of Fear and Hope* (Leiden: Brill E.J.) 1962, pp. 1-65.

6. Ibid.

Chapter 4

1. Watt, Montgomery W. *Freewill and Predestination in Early Islam* (London: Luzac) pp. 16-17; Patai, Raphael. *The Arab Mind* (New York: Scribner) 1976, p. 154.

2. Patai, *The Arab Mind,* p. 148.

3. Lane, Edward. W. *The Manners and Customs of Modern Egyptians* (London: Everyman's Library) n.d., pp. 477-478.

4. Haneef, Suzanne. *What Everybody Should Know About Islam and Muslims* (Chicago: Kazi) 1979, p. 39.

5. Patai, *The Arab Mind,* p. 58.

6. Smith, Jane I. and Y.Y. Haddad. *The Islamic Understanding of Death and Resurrection* (Albany: State University of New York Press) 1981, p. 107.

7. Haneef, Suzanne. *What Everbody Should Know,* p. 10.

8. Ibid., p. 14.

9. Maududi Abu A'la. *Toward Understanding Islam* (Beirut: Holy Koran Publishing House) 1980, pp. 17-19.

Chapter 5

1. Fisher, Mary Pat. *Living Religions* (NJ: Prentice-Hall) 1994, p. 187; John Bowker. *World Religions: The Great Faiths Explored and Explained* (Sydney: RD Press) 1997, p. 113.

2. Ma'sumian, Farnaz. *Life after Death: A Study of the Afterlife in World Religions* (Oxford: One World) 1995, p. 18.

3. Haneef, Suzanne. *What Everybody Should Know About Islam and Muslims* (Chicago: Kazi) 1979, p. 16.

4. Zakaria, Raphiq. *Muhammad and the Koran* (London: Penguin Books) 1991, p. 124.

Chapter 6

1. Smith, Jane I. and Y.Y. Haddad. *The Islamic Understanding of Death and Resurrection* (Albany: State University of New York Press) 1981, p. 43.

2. Izutsu, Toshihiko. *The Concept of Belief in Islamic Theology* (Tokyo: The Keio Institute of Cultural and Linguistic Studies) 1965, p. 37.

3. Smith, Jane I. and Y.Y. Haddad. *The Islamic Understanding of Death and Resurrection* (Albany: State University of New York Press) 1981, p. 105.

4. Ma'sumian, Farnaz. *Life after Death: A Study of the Afterlife in World Religions* (Oxford: One World) 1995, p. 76.

5. Coward, Harold (ed.). *Life after Death in World Religions* (New York: Orbis) 1997, p. 55.

Chapter 7

1. Smith, Jane I. and Y.Y. Haddad. *The Islamic Understanding of Death and Resurrection* (Albany: State University of New York Press) 1981, p. 66.

2. Ma'sumian, Farnaz. *Life after Death: A Study of the Afterlife in World Religions* (Oxford: One World) 1995, p. 71.

3. Smith and Haddad. *The Islamic Understanding,* p. 227.

4. Ma'sumian. *Life after Death: A Study,* p. 78.

5. Smith and Haddad. *The Islamic Understanding,* p. 69.

6. Ma'sumian. *Life after Death: A Study,* p. 79.

Chapter 8

1. Smith, Jane I. and Y.Y. Haddad. *The Islamic Understanding of Death and Resurrection* (Albany: State University of New York Press) 1981, pp. 72-73.

2. Ibid., pp. 77-78.

3. Latif, Syed Abdul: *The Mind Al-Qu'ran Builds* (Chicago: Kazi) 1983, pp. 192-193.

4. Ma'sumian, Farnaz. *Life after Death: A Study of the Afterlife in World Religions* (Oxford: One World) 1995, pp. 81-82.

5. Smith and Haddad, *Islamic Understanding,* p. 79.

6. Ibid., p. 185.

7. Iqbal, Muhammad. *The Reconstruction of Religious Thought in Islam* (Oxford: Oxford University Press) 1934, p. 123.

8. Khan, Hazrat Inayat. *The Sufi Message of Sufi Teaching,* Vol. 8 (London: Barry and Rockcliffe) 1963, pp. 182-183.

Chapter 9

1. Iqbal, Sir Muhammad. *The Reconstruction of Religious Thought in Islam* (Oxford: Oxford University Press) 1934, pp. 58-59.

2. Pike, Royston E. *Ethics of the Great Religions* (London: Watts) 1948, pp. 195-196.

3. Haneef, Suzanne. *What Everybody Should Know About Islam and Muslims* (Chicago: Kazi) 1979, pp. 43-46.

4. Adham, Abu Isaaq. "Why Our Du'as Are Not Accepted," in *Awake to the Call of Islam,* Vol. 2, No. 16, 1978.

Chapter 11

1. Brister, C.W. *Pastoral Care in the Church* (New York: Harper) 1964, p. 25.

2. Clebsch, W.A. and C.R. Jaekle. *Pastoral Care in Historical Perspective* (London: Harper and Torch) 1977, pp. 4-10.

3. Campbell, Alister V. *Rediscovering Pastoral Care* (London: Dayton, Longman, and Todd) 1981, p. 1.

4. Taylor, Michael H. *Learning to Care—Christian Perspectives in Pastoral Practice* (London: Society for the Propagation of Christian Knowledge) 1982, pp. 38-47.

Appendix 1

1. Smith, Jane I. and Y.Y. Haddad. *The Islamic Understanding of Death and Resurrection* (Albany: State University of New York Press) 1981, p. 182.

2. Padwick, Constance E. *Muslim Devotions* (London: Society for the Propagation of Christian Knowledge) 1961, p. 284.

Glossary

Adhan: A call to public prayer, usually from the minaret.

Ajal: Fixed term of the individual human life.

Allahu Akbar: "God is the most great."

Arafat: A vast barren plain near Mecca, the scene of one of the major observances of the Hajj when intercessory prayer is permissible.

Barzakh: Barrier, the time/place beyond the grave.

Bishmi'llah: In the name of Allah.

Dajjal: The anti-Christ.

Din: Religion, individual practical duties or response.

Fard: Obligatory or required religious duties.

Fiqh: Islamic jurisprudence.

Gehenna: Fire, originally the burning rubbish heaps outside Jerusalem.

Ghusl, (ghusal): Ritual washing.

Hadith: A narrative or communication. Recorded traditions of what Mohammed did and said.

Hajj: The annual pilgrimage to Mecca.

Halal: That which is permissible, lawful. e.g., food process.

Harem/Haram: Prohibited. The women's area.

Hijab: The covering dress of Muslim women.

Hijra: Migration. The migration of the Prophet to Medina C.E. 622, heralding the formation of the Islamic society.

Humdu'llah: Praise or thanks be to God.

N.B. In the transliteration of a word from Arabic to English there may be slight variations in spelling by different people. Transliteration depends upon skills in phonetics.

Iblis: The devil.

Id: Festival.

Imam: Religious leader.

Iman: Faith. Deep faith and trust in God.

Injil: The Christian Gospels.

Insha'llah: If God wills.

Isa: Jesus.

Islam: Submission. Total submission to Allah.

Jannah: "The Garden(s)" (i.e., in the future life).

Jihad: "Effort or earnest striving". . . within one's self, society, the world at large . . . for righteousness, against wrongdoing and oppression.

Jinn: Spirit. A species half demon/half human.

Ka'aba: Cube. The name of the central shrine in Mecca.

Kafir: Rejecters of Mohammed.

Kalima: Confession, particularly the first Pillar of Islam.

Khalifa: Successor or vice-regent. Successor of Mohammad. The "caliph" of Sunni Islam.

Kufr: Unbelief, infidelity. Rejection of the Prophet and his message.

Masjid: Lit. "Place of prostration" French . . . Mosque.

Maulvi: A Muslim doctor of law, learned man.

Mu'mim: Believer. A person of faith.

Nafs: Soul.

Purdah: The covering dress of Muslim women or their segregation from men outside the family.

Qiblah: Direction of prayer toward Mecca.

Ramadan: Ninth month of Islamic Calendar. Month of fasting.

Ruh: Spirit (of man).

Sa'a: The hour, the day Resurrection arrives.

Salat: Ritual prayer.

Shafa'a: Intercession.

Shi'a, Shi'ite: The members of the Islamic Community who follow the descendants of Ali and Fatima.

Shirk: Ascribing plurality to God.

Sunna(h): The recorded practice and ways of the Prophet. The Traditions.

Sunni: The majority party of the Islamic Community.

Taqba, Tawba: Repentance. Refers to the act of the sinner and God's response.

Taqwa: Consciousness of God, piety, Godliness, and devoutness.

Tawaf: The circumambulation of the Ka'aba, a pilgrimage duty.

Umma: Community, the "family" of Islam.

Umra: The lesser pilgrimage, made at any season.

Yathrib: Old name for Medina.

Zakat: Almsgiving, one of the obligatory duties.

Zamzam: The spring within the compound of the Mecca Mosque.

Bibliography

Ansari, F.R. *Islam and a Western Civilization* (Karachi: World Federation of Islamic Mission) 1967.

Ansari, F.R. *Philosophy of Worship in Islam* (Karachi: World Federation of Islamic Mission) 1964.

Bowker, John. *World Religions: The Great Faiths Explored and Explained* (Sydney: RD Press) 1997.

Brister, C. W. *Pastoral Care in the Church* (New York: Harper) 1964.

Campbell, Alistair V. *Rediscovering Pastoral Care* (London: Dayton, Longman, and Todd) 1981.

Clebsch, W.A. and C.R. Jaekle. *Pastoral Care in Historical Perspective* (London: Harper Torch Books) 1967.

Coward, Harold (ed.). *Life After Death in World Religions* (New York: Orbis) 1997.

Fisher, Mary Pat. *Living Religions* (New Jersey: Prentice-Hall) 1994.

Haneef, Suzanne. *What Everybody Should Know About Islam and Muslims* (Chicago: Kazi) 1979.

Hughes, T. P. *Dictionary of Islam* (Boise, ID: Allen and Co., Reprint) 1985.

Iqbal, Sir Mahommad. *The Reconstruction of Religious Thought in Islam* (Oxford: Oxford University Press) 1934.

Khan, Hazrat Inayat. *The Sufi Message of Sufi Teachings,* Vol. 8 (London: Barry and Rockliff) 1963.

Lane, Edward William. *The Manners and Customs of Modern Egyptians* (London: Everyman's Library Edition) n.d.

Ma'sumian, Farnaz. *Life After Death: A Study of the Afterlife in World Religions* (Oxford: One World) 1995.

Maudidi, Abu A'la. *Towards Understanding Islam* (Beirut: Holy Koran Publishing House) 1980.

McKane, William. *Al-Ghazali's Book of Fear and Hope* (Englewood Cliffs, NJ: Prentice-Hall) 1979.

Patai, Raphael. *The Arab Mind* (New York: Charles Scribner's Sons) 1976.

Pike, E. Royston. *Ethics of the Great Religions* (London: Watts) 1976.

Register, Ray G. Jr. *Dialogue and Interfaith Witness with Muslims* (Fort Washington: WEC Muslim Ministries) 1980.

Smith, Jane I. "The Understanding of Nafs and Ruh in Contemporary Muslim Considerations of the Nature of Sleep and Death," in *Muslim World* Vol. 69, No. 3, 1979.

Smith, Jane I. and Y.Y. Haddad. *The Islamic Understanding of Death and Resurrection* (Albany: State University of New York Press) 1981.

Taylor, Michael H. *Learning to Care: Christian Reflection on Pastoral Practice* (London: Society for the Propagation of Christian Knowledge) 1983.

Zakaria, Rafiq. *Muhammad and the Koran* (London: Penguin Books) 1991.

Index

Order Your Own Copy of
This Important Book for Your Personal Library!

PASTORAL CARE TO MUSLIMS
Building Bridges

_____in hardbound at $34.95 (ISBN: 0-7890-1476-9)

_____in softbound at $17.95 (ISBN: 0-7890-1477-7)

COST OF BOOKS_____

OUTSIDE USA/CANADA/
MEXICO: ADD 20%____

POSTAGE & HANDLING_____
(US: $4.00 for first book & $1.50
for each additional book)
Outside US: $5.00 for first book
& $2.00 for each additional book)

SUBTOTAL_____

in Canada: add 7% GST____

STATE TAX____
(NY, OH & MIN residents, please
add appropriate local sales tax)

FINAL TOTAL____
(If paying in Canadian funds,
convert using the current
exchange rate, UNESCO
coupons welcome.)

❑ **BILL ME LATER:** ($5 service charge will be added)
(Bill-me option is good on US/Canada/Mexico orders only;
not good to jobbers, wholesalers, or subscription agencies.)

❑ Check here if billing address is different from
shipping address and attach purchase order and
billing address information.

Signature_____

❑ **PAYMENT ENCLOSED: $**_____

❑ **PLEASE CHARGE TO MY CREDIT CARD.**

❑ Visa ❑ MasterCard ❑ AmEx ❑ Discover
❑ Diner's Club ❑ Eurocard ❑ JCB

Account #_____

Exp. Date_____

Signature_____

Prices in US dollars and subject to change without notice.

NAME_____

INSTITUTION_____

ADDRESS_____

CITY_____

STATE/ZIP_____

COUNTRY_____ COUNTY (NY residents only)_____

TEL_____ FAX_____

E-MAIL_____

May we use your e-mail address for confirmations and other types of information? ❑ Yes ❑ No
We appreciate receiving your e-mail address and fax number. Haworth would like to e-mail or fax special
discount offers to you, as a preferred customer. **We will never share, rent, or exchange your e-mail address
or fax number.** We regard such actions as an invasion of your privacy.

Order From Your Local Bookstore or Directly From
The Haworth Press, Inc.
10 Alice Street, Binghamton, New York 13904-1580 • USA
TELEPHONE: 1-800-HAWORTH (1-800-429-6784) / Outside US/Canada: (607) 722-5857
FAX: 1-800-895-0582 / Outside US/Canada: (607) 722-6362
E-mail: getinfo@haworthpressinc.com
PLEASE PHOTOCOPY THIS FORM FOR YOUR PERSONAL USE.
www.HaworthPress.com

BOF00